Traditional Life in Shetland

James R. Nicolson

ROBERT HALE · LONDON

© James R. Nicolson 1978, 1990
First published in Great Britain 1978
Reprinted 1978, 1983
First paperback edition 1990

ISBN 0 7090 4033 4

The right of James R. Nicolson to be identified as
author of this work has been asserted by him
in accordance with the Copyright, Designs and
Patents Act 1988.

Robert Hale Limited
Clerkenwell House
Clerkenwell Green
London EC1R 0HT

Printed in Great Britain by
St Edmundsbury Press Limited, Bury St Edmunds, Suffolk
and bound by WBC Bookbinders Limited

Contents

Glossary of Dialect Words not explained in the text 9

1 The Islands 17

2 The People 26

3 The Dialect 37

4 The Croft 50

5 House and Home 71

6 Special Skills 87

7 The Work of the Sea 102

8 Superstitions and Folklore 124

9 Shetland's Calendar 140

10 The Cycle of Life 155

11 The Dawn of Modern Times 168

12 Shetland's Heritage 178

Bibliography 198

Index 201

Acknowledgements

Many people have contributed unwittingly towards the writing of this book. From my childhood days I have been fortunate to have among my friends and relatives people with a profound knowledge of life as it was lived in Shetland in the latter part of the nineteenth century. Over the past four or five years I have gleaned a great deal of information from the files of *The Shetland Times* which appeared in 1872 and is still going strong and of *The Shetland News* which was published between 1885 and 1963. I am grateful to Mr Basil Wishart, Editor of *The Shetland Times* and to Dr T. M. Y. Manson, formerly Editor of *The Shetland News* for their co-operation. Again Shetland is fortunate in having a well-stocked Shetland Room in the County Library and I am grateful to the librarians, Mr George Longmuir and his successor Mr John Hunter for their assistance at all times.

Most of all I am indebted to the late Mr Tom Henderson, curator of Shetland Museum and to his successor, Mr Andrew Williamson, who contributed information concerning the extremities of this island group. The former had a deep knowledge of the parish of Dunrossness while the latter was born and brought up in the island of Yell. They kindly read my manuscript, pointed out several errors and omissions and without their help it would have been extremely difficult to write this book. Finally I wish to place on record my appreciation of the help given by the late Mr George M. Nelson of Veensgarth. His death in December 1976 robbed the islands of one of their most noted authorities on all aspects of traditional life.

J. R. N.

Illustrations

Between pages 64 and 65

1   A typical late nineteenth-century croft
2   Shetland breed of cattle
3   Cutting oats with a corn hook
4   An old-style wedding
5   House interior
6   Cutting peats with a tushkar
7   Using ponies to carry peats in the island of Fetlar
8   A peat carrier, knitting as she walks
9   Water mills at Huxter
10 Making a straw kishie
11 Herring fleet leaving Lerwick in the 1890s
12 A steam drifter discharging her catch
13 Sixerns at Fedeland

PICTURE CREDITS

C. J. Williamson: 6. All other photographs supplied by th Shetland Library and Museum

Glossary of Dialect Words
not explained in the text

aa—all
aalie pootie—a piglet reared at the fireside
aald—old
abune—above
aet—eat
ain—own
almark—a sheep which continuously breaks through enclosures
an—and
anidder—another
ask—haze
athin—within

bane—bone
bate—a small bundle especially of straw
bent—marram grass
bid—a small length of line by which a hook is attached to a long line
bigg—build
blaa—blow
blugga bane—collar bone of a halibut
bogel—a kind of oatcake
boo—bend
brak—break
brand iron—gridiron
branks—a triangular collar of wood fastened round an almark's neck
    to prevent it penetrating a fence. Originally a horse halter.
brigstanes—flagstones laid as a pavement in front of a house
brokken—broken
brook—broke
Broonie—a domestic trow or fairy
brukkin—crushing

brünie—a cake
büddie—a basket—usually the kind carried by a fisherman
bül—a hollow used by animals for shelter; also a verb—to make animals comfortable
burn—a stream
bussom—a besom

caa—drive (sheep or whales)
caird—card (prepare wool for spinning)
cald—cold
cøl—cool
crø—an enclosure—especially one where sheep are penned
crook—an S-shaped iron hook above the fire on which cooking pots were hung
crook bauk—a beam of wood above the fire from which were suspended the links and the crook
cüid(e)—a three-year-old saithe
curldodie—the spotted orchid

da—the
daaty—a term of endearment for a child
dan—then
dat—that
dee—die
dir—their
dis—this
droo—a type of seaweed that grows to a great length

een—one
enyoch—enough
ess—ash

fael—a thick slab of turf
fan—found
fedder—feather
fir—for
fit—foot
flaa—thin cover of heather and grass pared off for roofing
flee—fly
flit—to move to a new house; to move a tethered animal to fresh pasture
floss—rushes

fok—folk
foo—how
fu—full

gaeslin—gosling
gadder—gather
girnal—large box for storing meal
girse—grass
gloy—straw
gorsties—boundaries between fields
gref—the floor or pit of a peat bank
grice—a piglet
grind—a gate
gruel tree—a porridge stick
guizer—one who attends a party or other function disguised with
  a mask or fancy dress
gutter—mud
gyaain trang taegidder—courting (going strong together)
gyit—get

haaf—the deep sea
haet—hot
hain—save
hairst—harvest
hallo—a sheaf
halvers—joint ownership
harns—brains
hedder—heather
hedder cowe—a clump of heather
hert stane—hearth
hinnie spot—a triangular piece of wood joining a boat's gunwales
  either to the stem or to the stern
hinniwir—an edible seaweed
hoid—hide
holm—an islet
hüve—throw

ida—in the

jøst or *juist*—just

kame—a comb
kappie—an anchor stone for a fishing line

ken—know
kent—known
kirn—churn
kirn milk—a soft cheese produced in the churn after the removal
    of the butter
kirvie—a bundle (especially of rushes)
kishie—a large basket carried on one's back
klaag—a commotion (of birds)
klibber—a wooden saddle to which baskets were attached
kline—spread
kokkilurie—a daisy
kollie—a simple type of lamp
krook—an earthenware bottle
kye—cattle

laach—laugh
laek—like
lane—self (as in *me lane, its lane*)
leep—to soften (bait) by heating in water
lightenin tree—a device for altering the separation of the millstones
lioom—an oily film on water
looder—a shelf-like table
looder horn—the horn of an ox used as a fog horn by fishermen
lowse—loose
lug—ear
lum—an opening in the roof to allow smoke to escape (the name
    later applied to the chimney)

maa—a seagull
maet—food
maun—must
Maunsie—familiar form of Christian name Magnus
me—my
me lane—myself
midder—mother
moor—to drift (snow)
moor up—to become enveloped in a snowdrift
moorit—brown (sheep or wool)
muckle—large
müld—earth or peat mould

neb—a beak
nedder—neither

nev—a fist

njuggle—a supernatural creature at times resembling a pony once believed to frequent stream and lochs

oo—wool

owsin room—the compartment in an open boat where sea water is bailed out

paek—pick; *da green paek*—the first green grass in voar

peerie—small

pernyim—prim

perskeet—fastidious

piltock—a young saithe when it is two years old

pit—put

poan—a slab of turf cut for roofing

pock—a dip net

purl—poke

quern—a small, hand-operated mill

raep—rope stretched across the room for supporting articles to be dried

redd—to clear (as a tangled line)

reek—smoke

reestit mutton—salted and dried mutton

restin chair—a wooden settle

rig—a field

rigg—the backbone

rivlins—slippers made of cowhide or sealskin

rød—fine rain or drizzle also the outpourings of a talkative person

rodd—a road

roo—to remove wool by pulling gently as opposed to clipping

rooder—barnacles (sometimes applied to all types of growth on a rock that lies below high water mark)

roog—a heap

sae—a tub

sain—to protect from evil by making the sign of the cross

sanna—shall not

scattald—the common grazings

scoom—to skim (fish in a pot)

shaest—to chase

shappin tree—a potato masher

shoard—support for a boat on a beach
shøre—sheared (past tense of verb to shear)
shoormil—the edge of the sea
shun—a small lake
shün(e)—soon
sid—a husk of oats
sillock—young saithe under two years old
simmer—summer
simmond—a home-made rope made from straw, heather, etc.
sixern—a six-oared fishing boat
skekler—a guizer in a special dress of straw
skeo—a stone 'larder' in which meat and fish were preserved in an unsalted state
skroo—a stack of oats
skudler—the leader of a band of skeklers
skyle—a wooden board positioned on the windward side of the lum to assist the smoke in escaping through the opening
slap—a hole in a dry stone wall
smirsleen—an edible shellfish (*Mya truncata*)
snet—wipe (one's nose)
soo—sow (female pig)
sparl—the final section of a sheep's or cow's intestine, stuffed with minced meat, soaked in pickle then dried above the fire
spunk—a glowing particle of peat or wood
stank—a ditch
stoor—dust
støl—stole
stirleen—a starling
süne—see *shüne*
swaabie—great black backed gull

taat—a thread especially a thick thread used in making taatit rugs
tang—seaweed
tap—top
tattie—a potato
tedder—a tether
tee—a leg of mutton
tig—to beg
tirl—the mill wheel
tøn—a tune
trow—a troll
trowe—through
trucket—trampled underfoot

tushkar—a peat-cutting spade
twartree—two or three

unken—strange

vaigin—travelling
veeshon—vision
voar—springtime
voe—a long sea inlet
vooer—a suitor

waar—a type of seaweed with broad leaves
whirm—vanish quickly
wid—wood
wilsom—misleading
winder—wonder
wir—our
wirs—ours
wye—way

yield—unmated
yoag—a horse mussel

Zetland—until 1974 the official name for the county

I

The Islands

Since the discovery of North Sea oil Shetland has assumed a new importance in the eyes of the British public, while parts of the islands themselves have been transformed to prepare them for their new role. Symbols of the oil age are the helicopters flying from Sumburgh airport, the powerful service vessels casting off from their bases with supplies for the oil rigs, and the giant storage tanks, the flare stacks and the tanker loading jetties of Sullom Voe. But underneath this veneer of modern technology there is abundant evidence of a long and fascinating history, when the islands had to depend on their own resources, and a distinctive way of life evolved, adapted to a unique environment. Unfortunately, the picture is marred by a period of oppression and cruel examples of man's inhumanity to man.

Shetland's land was poor and agriculture difficult, but by adding the resources of the sea a living was possible. This fusion of two occupations forms a double-stranded thread that runs right through the history of these islands from prehistoric times. For many hundreds of years the Shetlander has been a fisherman with a croft.

The painstaking work of the archaeologist has shown how a succession of peoples came and established their own pattern of living. Neolithic man was followed in turn by users of bronze and iron; men who built the so-called wheel houses succeeded those who built the brochs—those mysterious castles that marked the high point in the art of dry-stone building almost 2,000 years ago.

Few traces remain of the Celtic people who lived here for

hundreds of years, although the sites of early churches at places such as Papil and St Ninian's Isle testify to the faith and devotion of those early Christians. At the last-named locality there was made one of the most important archaeological discoveries in the whole of Britain—a collection of silver brooches, plates and goblets fashioned with great skill and exhibiting a man-made beauty such as the islands have never seen since. For the Celtic stream of culture was cut short by the Viking invasion of the eighth and ninth centuries, and it was the Norsemen who laid the foundations of a highly practical way of life that continued until well into the present century.

The warriors were followed by the settlers—men and women who came across the North Sea in their thousands to continue their own traditions in their adopted country. They gave a name to every hill and knoll, every loch, burn and marsh, every headland, ness and point, every bight, voe and wick, even to the holms and stacks standing in the sea and to the rocks and reefs under the sea. They took possession of these islands to such an extent that it has been suggested since that the earlier Celtic inhabitants must have been entirely obliterated. However, the Norse name for a Pict—*Pettr*—survives in several places. Just as the name Pettland, an old name for Scotland, survives in the form of Pentland Firth, so the word *Pettr* continues in Shetland in places names such as Pettadale and Pettawater on the boundary of Tingwall and Delting.

Perhaps the Picts were not exterminated but were instead absorbed into a predominantly Norse community. No doubt old people would cling to their own way of life in their earth houses as far away as possible from the homes of the incomers. On the steep rocky coastline of the east side of Unst there is a slope hidden from the view of a person standing on the ridge above, and reached only by a difficult path down the cliff. It is known as Pettasmog, which later researchers suggest may have been originally *Petta Smuga*—the Picts' hiding place.

During the centuries of Norse rule that followed, Shetland never shared the status that Orkney held as the seat of the earldom of Orkney and Shetland. Only occasionally did the earls visit Shetland, although they no doubt broke their journeys here, and on one occasion Earl Rognvald was shipwrecked at Gulberwick. Instead we find the names of ordinary Norse farmers and fishermen perpetuated in Shetland's place names—personal names such as Balti, Egill, Huni, Kolr, Vemundr, Svein and Hildir, each of which is commemorated today in the names of small islands, while the name, Grim, is perpetuated in Grimista (Grim's farmstead) on the outskirts of Lerwick.

For more than 500 years life continued peacefully. Land was held under the Norwegian system of udal tenure which, unlike feudal tenure, carried no obligations such as military or personal service to a superior. Land was the property of the first improver and a settler could enclose as much land for improvement as he required. Shetland was governed by a magistrate known as the foude who derived his authority from the king of Norway. The islands were divided into ten or eleven districts each governed by an inferior foude assisted by a group of officers known as ranselmen. Once a year there took place the great assembly of the Alting at Tingwall where the islands' laws were enacted.

A change came in the thirteenth century with a weakening of Norwegian influence under the growing interest of Scotland. The Norse line of earls was replaced by the Scottish line of Angus, which was in turn replaced by the lines of Strathearne and St Clair. But still Shetland continued to owe allegiance to Norway until 1469, when a Danish king, short of money for his daughter's dowry, was forced to pledge these islands to the Scottish crown.

The period following the transfer is still imperfectly understood by historians. The most eventful period was that following 1564, when Robert Stewart held the islands as Earl of Orkney and Lord of Shetland, being succeeded in 1593 by his son Patrick. If the traditional view of those men is correct, they ruled as ruthless tyrants who confiscated much of the udallers' lands. Robert Stewart built a mansion at Sumburgh, while Patrick built the castle whose ruins still dominate the village of Scalloway. The Stewart line was brought to an end with the execution of Earl Patrick at Edinburgh in 1615, and soon afterwards the islands were annexed to Scotland.

The removal of the Stewarts left the way open for the rise of the landowners, many of whom had come to Shetland as churchmen, but who exchanged their hopes of a reward in the next world for the immediate opportunities they found here.

All the evils perpetrated by colonialists in other parts of the world were experienced in Shetland as the new class of landlords established their supremacy over the original inhabitants. By 1700 Shetland was in the hands of a few Scottish lairds, while the bulk of Shetlanders had ceased to be small landowners supporting themselves on their own farms and had become mere tenants cultivating a patch of land for which they paid rent to incomers.

Along with the Stewarts and the churchmen, a great number of ordinary Scottish people had settled in Shetland, becoming crofters and fishermen like the descendants of the Norse. Nothing shows more clearly the importance of these two racial elements than a study of island surnames. In Norse times surnames were rare—a man was given a first name such as Sigurd, Olaf or Thorfinn and sometimes an adjective to describe some physical trait.

Then came the age of Christianity, and, as befits baptized Christians, each man was given a Christian name, generally that of a saint such as John, Peter, Andrew or Thomas. Surnames were still rare, but a man took as an appellation the Christian name of his father with the suffix 'son'. Thus John, son of Thomas, became John Thomason, while his sons would in turn all share the surname Johnson. This was the Norse system of patronymics which continued until the middle of the nineteenth century, and is still marked by the large number of island surnames that end with 'son'. With the Reformation some additional Christian names—generally good, dependable Old Testament names such as Adam, Gideon and Hosea—were brought into use and were again subjected to the system of patronymics.

Among the Scottish incomers, however, fixed surnames were a characteristic that tended to separate them from the original inhabitants. Among the earliest Scottish landowners were the numerous branches of the Sinclair family—Sinclairs of Houss, Sandness, Brew, Scalloway, Ness, Havera and several more. During the sixteenth and seventeenth centuries there arrived such typically Scottish surnames as Mitchell, Mowat and Gifford, many of them introduced by clergymen. Andrew Edmonstone was minister of Mid and South Yell in 1599, while Peter Simsone was reader in Whalsay and Out Skerries between

1579 and 1589. John Gifford was reader at Northmavine in 1567, while Gilbert Mowat was minister there in 1615. Andrew Wishart was vicar of Sandsting and Aithsting in 1543, while John Sutherland was reader there in 1585. It is surprising that in many cases these surnames remain closely associated with their respective districts.

The influx of Scottish immigrants continued, and in subsequent centuries more and more surnames were added to the islands' list. The surname Dowell (pronounced Dool) used to be particularly common around West Burrafirth, and according to Dr Hibbert, those who hold this surname are descendants of a soldier named McDougall who arrived in the pay of Oliver Cromwell when his troops garrisoned Scalloway Castle.

Within a remarkably short time the two elements, Scottish and Norse, had become fused into a race of crofters and fishermen. The earliest landed families, the Sinclairs, no longer possessed their lands, and they too became crofters and fishermen, hounded by new lairds and chastened by new ministers. There was little time for considering whether your or your neighbour's surname was Norwegian or Scottish. Life was difficult and hunger never far away. It just took one poor fishing season or one crop failure to produce extreme hardship whether your name was Mowat or Manson.

With the rise of the lairds the lot of ordinary people deteriorated. Where previously it had been sufficient to produce food to sustain themselves and their families, they now had the added burden of an annual rent to be raised; and since the lairds found work degrading the tenants had to cultivate their masters' farms, take in their crops, cut, cure and carry home their peats, repair their houses and provide a succession of presents of meat, fish and poultry for banquets at the big house.

During this long period of misrule by the lairds, the one bright spot was trade with the Continent. Each summer hundreds of Dutch sailing busses fished the rich herring grounds east of Shetland. They used the wide and empty stretch of water between Bressay and the Mainland of Shetland as a point of assembly, waiting until 24th June—the Feast of St John the Baptist—which was the agreed date for the start of the herring season. The fishermen came ashore for exercise and to trade with the country people, and it was as a direct result of the contact with the Dutch that a settlement of trading stalls was erected in the seventeenth century on the shore of Bressay Sound, around the little bay known as Ler Wick. In spite of opposition from the authorities of the day, the settlement continued to grow, and by the end of the seventeenth century Lerwick had replaced Scalloway as the largest village in Shetland.

Surprisingly, the herring shoals were not exploited by Shetland's fishermen. Instead they fished with handlines for ling and cod. The earliest fish merchants were Hanseatic traders from North Germany who arrived in May each year, rented beaches and sheds from the local landowners and purchased the catches of the local fishermen for salting and drying before being shipped in autumn to the Continent. In fact little money changed hands, since the fishermen merely bartered their catch for hempen cloth, salt, flour and articles of clothing besides tobacco, 'corn waters' and other luxuries otherwise unobtainable in Shetland.

The activities of the Hanseatic merchants declined in the later decades of the seventeenth century and ceased altogether about 1712, the last straw being the Salt Tax introduced by the British government to encourage British shipping. But the fishing industry did not decline since the landowners stepped in as merchants to fill the vacuum left by the traders of Hamburg and Bremen, and under the management of the lairds it developed rapidly until it became the main activity of the islands and the backbone of their entire economic structure.

The whole system of land tenure changed, leases being given for one year only and including the stipulation that the tenant must fish for his laird. If caught selling part of his catch to another merchant the tenant could expect to be given forty days' notice to vacate his house and croft. It was a good bargain from the landlord's point of view, since in addition to the rent of his tenant he received his fish at a low price. Again the tenant was bound to purchase all the provisions required by him and his family from the laird's shop, and naturally the laird had a profit on that too. Should a young man try to seek a change from fishing by signing on as a hand on a vessel from Hull or Dundee for a trip to the Arctic whaling grounds, the family often had their rent raised to compensate the laird for the loss of a fisherman.

The emphasis shifted even more from the land towards the sea, and since it was advantageous for the landowners to have as many fishermen as possible on their estates, early marriages were encouraged and the crofts were subdivided to enable two families to exist where only one could survive before. Agriculture suffered through lack of attention, while the nature of the tenancy gave the family no incentive to improve their croft, since they could be turned out at short notice. Under the stimulus of the fishing industry the population of the islands increased from a little over 22,000 at the beginning of the century to almost 32,000 in 1861—far too many for the islands to support on their meagre resources.

Fishing tenures began to be relaxed on some estates about 1830, although most tenants continued to fish as before, since there was no other opportunity for employment in Shetland, selling their catches to the new fish merchants who were starting business all over the islands. In many estates, however, fishing was still of supreme importance and the system of fishing tenure was retained. Again some lairds shifted their emphasis from fish to sheep, following the example of their fellow landlords on the mainland of Scotland, and their tenants were merely an embarrassment standing between them and the green fields that they required as pasture for their flocks of sheep. However, it was a simple matter to evict them, since the tenants had no security other than the necessity of forty days' notice to quit.

Evictions were not carried out on such an extensive scale as in parts of the Highlands, but here too there were many examples of the inhumanity of the period. Among the first clearances were those of Fetlar in the 1820s, when a large number of families were forced to leave the island. The fertile valley of Weisdale was substantially 'cleared' in 1850, and the fields cultivated for hundreds of years were left untilled for the benefit of the Black Face and the Cheviot.

In 1862 a new phase began with the arrival in the islands of Mr John Walker, agent for Major Cameron of Garth, who persuaded his employer to adopt the principle of clearance on an extensive scale. Mr Walker was especially covetous of the scattalds, the wide stretches of common grazing in the hills upon which the crofters depended as pasture for their sheep. He realized that the hills would be ideal for the establishment of large sheep farms, and the crofters were simply told that they would no longer be allowed to graze their livestock there.

This had the same effect as eviction since without the scattalds the crofter could not keep a sufficient number of sheep and cattle, and many more families were forced to join the stream of emigrants to the Colonies and the Dominions. At Mr Walker's instigation large parts of Delting and the island of Yell were cleared of crofters and formed into sheep runs. The people did not realize that Mr Walker was thinking only of their well-being, since he later claimed that he removed the scattalds from crofting use because they were of no use to the people and were actually doing them harm.

In the 1870s there came another change when the landowners realized that they could make the best of both worlds. They could remove most of the scattald and enclose it for sheep farms, but they could leave just enough for the people to keep a few sheep and cattle to enable them to continue to live more or less as before, and to remain as fishermen selling their catches to their landlord. In many cases the people were allowed to keep a certain number of sheep on the scattald at the payment of, say, a shilling a head each year.

A great deal of information concerning life at this time was assembled in the Minutes of the Truck Commission, which visited Shetland in 1872 to investigate the growing volume of complaints and especially the relationship between tenants and their landlords and merchants. It is clear that some estates were managed more humanely than others. Tenants of the Earl of Zetland apparently had greater security than others and retained a considerable amount of the scattalds for their own use. At the other end of the scale was the estate described by crofter Laurence Jarmson. He complained of high rents, since about 1870 the laird had suddenly increased all the rents in that district by about one-third. When the tenants complained, the laird produced a document offering to reduce the rent of those who agreed to bind themselves to him as fishermen. Those who signed had their rent reduced by about five shillings.

Fortunately an enlightened era was just around the corner,

for with the passing of the Crofters Holdings (Scotland) Act of 1886 the crofters received that most basic of human rights—security of tenure. In addition they were granted the right to receive compensation for improvements carried out to their croft during the period of tenancy should they decide to vacate it. It did not go unnoticed that a Liberal government was in power at the time and for most of the succeeding ninety years Shetlanders have returned a Liberal member of parliament to Westminster.

2

The People

At the beginning of the nineteenth century Shetland was still a remote northern region virtually unknown to people in the rest of Britain. Links with the Scottish Mainland were provided by sailing smacks that sailed five or six times a year between Lerwick and Leith, while inter-island communications were provided as required by sixerns—open fishing boats rowed by six men. Naturally the more remote islands were cut off from the rest of Shetland for months at a time. On the Mainland of Shetland the situation was little better. Roads were practically non-existent apart from a three-mile stretch constructed between Lerwick and Tingwall by one of the more progressive of the landlords. Each little port traded direct with the Continent but with other parts of Shetland there was surprisingly little contact.

At this time the only medical practitioner in the islands was Dr Laurence Edmondston of Unst, and his practice was carried on in a most unusual manner. A member of some laird's family would fall ill, and a sixern would be despatched with an urgent request for assistance. The doctor would pack his medicine chest and start on his long journey, seldom knowing when he would see his home again. He might stay for several weeks under the laird's roof, and inevitably all those in the neighbourhood who had ailments would come to him for treatment.

Although unknown to the British public Shetland did not escape the notice of the Royal Navy. At this time Britain was at war with France and there was a constant demand for seamen. Shetland was an obvious target for attention, since with the development of the fishing industry every man and boy was

skilled in handling a boat and well acquainted with the com-
plexities of sails and cordage, knots and splices.

The Press Gang scoured the islands, seizing every able-bodied
man they could find and herding them like animals on board
men-of-war. They would enter houses at night and haul men
out of their beds; fishermen at sea had an added danger to face.
Hairbreadth escapes were numerous, and the events of this
troubled period have made a great contribution to the folklore
of these islands.

Whaling ships were overhauled on their return from the
Arctic, and all except the fixed complement were pressed into
service. It was the practice for those vessels to leave their home
ports in England and Scotland with sufficient men to sail them,
while extra hands required for whaling operations were engaged in Orkney and Shetland. Many a Shetlander, looking forward to seeing his wife and children after an absence of many
months among the ice floes of the Arctic, never saw his family
again. Instead he found himself in another ship, called upon to
fight the French, and many Shetlanders were killed in action or
died in a French prison.

Some lived to return home when peace was restored. The
story is still told of how two ex-prisoners returned to their
homes at Quarff, and how in memory of their ordeal one renamed his croft Casho (from the French word '*cachot*' meaning prison) while the other renamed his Purgatory. Another
prisoner, Anton Dowell, returned to his home near West Burrafirth scarred for life with the marks of iron chains deeply worn
into his wrists and ankles. It is not surprising that when peace
was declared it was welcomed as enthusiastically in Shetland
as anywhere in Britain.

But peace did not bring an alleviation of Shetland's other
problems, many of which seemed to get worse. Life continued
to revolve round the village shop, usually owned by the laird
or by the tacksman who farmed the rents. The fishermen's
catches were landed on the merchant's beach, and the surplus
products of the croft were carried to the shop, where a nominal value was credited against the value of merchandise bought.
The laird was still the owner of the crofter's land, his house,
and his boat, while he was the unofficial banker for the whole
district. This gave the laird tremendous control over the lives

of his tenants and left the latter in a state little better than slavery.

The 1840s marked a grim chapter in the history of these islands. The previous decade had seen the start of a herring fishery which promised to bring prosperity to fisherman and merchant alike, but a succession of poor seasons led to the collapse of this new venture and the failure of the fishermen's bank at Lerwick, when many men lost their entire savings. Worse was to follow with a series of crop failure between 1846 and 1849 which gave the name 'The Hungry Forties' to the entire decade. To prevent famine the British government, through the Board for the Relief of Highland Destitution, began a programme of road-building, the workmen being paid in meal. Looking back at this era, the one bright spot in the otherwise unrelieved gloom was the construction of a chain of roads along the central spine of the Mainland and in the island of Yell.

In spite of so many difficulties, the spirit of the people remained unbroken. They learned to laugh at adversity and to accept poverty as part of their lot. When they had managed to pay the laird his annual exaction they were free to get on with the real purpose of life—making a living for themselves and their families, looking after their cattle and sheep, repairing and re-thatching their stone-walled cottages, cutting and curing their peats and making most of their own clothing. As they sat around a blazing peat fire on a winter's night, the men repairing fishing lines or making straw baskets, the women knitting or spinning their wool and all of them laughing and chatting as they worked, the laird seemed a remote figure sitting austere and lonely in his cold and cheerless hall. Although far from satisfied with their lot, few of them would have accepted his riches in exchange for the wealth of friendship which they themselves enjoyed.

Life was hard during the summer, the men away for long periods as they followed their dangerous calling, and during this time an added burden fell on the women, since they had to tend the crops and look after the animals in addition to their normal household duties. But when the crops were gathered in and the fishing boat was hauled ashore for the winter, life assumed a more leisurely pace which not even the rigours of a severe winter could upset. Winter was the time for merrymaking—even marriages were usually reserved for this season and the wedding celebrations that might continue for two or three days and nights helped to brighten what would have been otherwise a dark time of year. Then in midwinter came Yule with its twenty-four days of celebrations, and on almost every one of those nights a dance would be held in someone's barn.

The musical instrument was the fiddle, which had been introduced in the eighteenth century, replacing the older Norse two-stringed instrument known as the gue. The fiddle became so popular that in 1808 it was estimated that one in ten of the population could play it. Shetlanders were skilled at composing tunes as well as playing, and each district had its own reel tunes. Many were learned at sea, since each Greenland whaler carried at least one fiddler to entertain the crew, and in this way Shetlanders brought back Scottish, English and Irish fiddle tunes which they usually altered unconsciously into a typically Shetland form.

There were some outstanding fiddlers—men like John Goudie of Levenwick, usually known as 'Mad John Gadie' since an unfortunate accident had injured his brain and had led to periods of insanity. Another famous fiddler was Peter Hunter of Bressay, who died in 1836 in the Davis Straits on board the whaler *Swan* when she was trapped in the ice and forced to spend the winter there. And apart from the experts there were scores of men whose services were in great demand at rants or dances and hundreds more who played solely to entertain themselves and their families.

As a rule the islanders were extremely honest and law-abiding, but there were occasions when the law was bent slightly to suit the special island situation. The people tended to believe that an owner's interest in a ship and its cargo ended the moment it struck the rocks, and although no effort was spared to assist the survivors of a shipwreck, the ship and its cargo were subject to the principle of first come, first served. Haste was essential, since the proprietor of the ground on which the stranding occurred and the representatives of the crown also considered that they had certain salvage rights.

Shipwrecks came under the category of godsends—things that did not happen in accordance with a predictable pattern, but which when they did occur offered temporary relief in the struggle against poverty. This attitude was, perhaps surprisingly, shared by the parish ministers. In 1744 Rev John Mill of Dunrossness willingly moved out of his lodgings to accommodate shipwrecked officers from the Swedish East Indiaman *Stockholm*, but a few years later he called the wreck of a Danish vessel a godsend since it provided timber for his church.

Other godsends were the caaing whales, which stranded in great numbers during the nineteenth century, and boat hires. Dr Hibbert, a visitor of 1816, bemoaned the fact that a voyage in Shetland was spoilt by the behaviour of the boat's crew, as having agreed on the charge before the journey began they continued to bargain for an increased rate as the journey proceeded, taking advantage of the passenger's rather weak bargaining position. But Dr Hibbert had reason to congratulate the people on their honesty, since while staying at Unifirth he lost the keys of his trunks and his belongings were seen by more than twenty people over the space of several days, yet nothing was taken.

In their attitude to smuggling the people also bent the rules a little. Smuggling was carried out by all sectors of the community, since it was considered neither dishonest or immoral to defraud H.M. Customs of the levy which they considered their due. There was plenty of opportunity for smuggling with hundreds of Dutch busses arriving every summer to prosecute the herring fishery, their crews eager to procure a little pocket money or to exchange a few cigars or a bottle of gin for eggs and fresh meat. When Lerwick developed as a seaport in the eighteenth century, an integral part of nearly every private house and private jetty was a secret compartment where smuggled goods could be hidden away.

Many of Shetland's fishermen had their own means of securing contraband. During most of the nineteenth century dozens of cod smacks set out from Shetland each spring to fish the banks around the Faroe Islands. It became customary on the second voyage to put into Thorshavn to do some shopping— the shopping list being confined to brandy and tobacco for the use of the crew and their friends back home. Over the years thousands of gallons of spirits and tons of tobacco were smuggled into Shetland in spite of the efforts of the Customs officers

ashore and of the revenue cutter that patrolled the approaches
to these islands. If possible the smacks would time their arrival
at Shetland to the few hours of darkness, and by daylight the
cargo would have been secreted in peat stacks, barns and outhouses. From all over Shetland came stories of how the Customs officers were outwitted. One from Levenwick relates how
following a tip-off a raid was made on a house there. The
officers were invited to search the house but were requested to
be as quick as possible, since the good wife was in labour.
When the men had left the house the woman was safely delivered of the parcel of tobacco on which she had been lying.

Smuggling remained an acceptable practice to the very end of
the nineteenth century, but by this time the increasing vigilance of the Customs' officers made it an extremely risky business. In August 1886 two Dutch vessels deeply laden with
contraband, and caught red-handed making a transaction inside
territorial waters at Dunrossness, were seized and taken to
Lerwick, where the crews were brought before the Sheriff. The
case received a great deal of publicity, and from the accounts in
the local newspapers it was quite clear where the Shetlanders'
sympathy lay. The court was packed with people, and when it
was agreed that the Dutchmen should be released on bail there
was an immediate outburst of applause 'which was instantly
suppressed, His Honour remarking that such exhibitions were
very improper'.

As early as the 1790s the parish ministers, writing in the *Old
Statistical Account*, were complaining that too much drink was
being consumed by their parishioners. The minister of Unst
went as far as to suggest that a suppression of smuggling would
be advantageous to improving morals. An improvement seems
to have taken place within the next few decades, for in the
New Statistical Account compiled in 1841 the minister of Sandsting and Aithsting declared that there was no propensity in
the people generally to indulge to excess in 'spiritous liquors',
while in Unst there was a temperance society with 300 members. Thereafter every visitor to these islands seemed obsessed
with the question of whether or not the Shetlanders drank too
much, nor were they agreed in their verdict. In 1881 John R.
Tudor claimed that the success of the Orcadians and Shet-

landers in the Mercantile Marine was due to their temperate, if not teetotal, habits.

It is unlikely that the Shetlanders were at any time more immoral than people elsewhere in Britain, but the lairds and ministers used to believe that this was the case. Every calamity and every poor season or crop failure was regarded as the wrath of God upon a sinful people, and there were frequent fast days set aside to avert divine anger. At a great meeting of the lairds in 1775 they accused the people in general of all manner of vices including Sabbath breaking, cursing, lying, fornication, malice, covetousness, drunkenness and 'abominable feuds between husband and wife'. These they attributed to neglect of religion and education, a fulness of bread and indifference by the civil officers and ministers to their duty.

To overcome their problems they had the ranselmen and the elders of each district combined into a Society for the Regulation of Servants and Reformation of Manners, with wide powers of spying upon their neighbours and reporting minor misdemeanours. One of the Acts decreed that 'no person . . . . . . travel by sea or land upon the Sabbath day . . . except in works of necessity and mercy'. Again each person 'sitting at home from the kirk on the Sabbath day, or withdrawing from divine service without a good reason' should be fined thirty shillings (Scots) for each offence.

These acts were abandoned towards the end of the eighteenth century, and Dr Hibbert, writing in 1816, commented that in spite of this the people were 'honest, enterprising, industrious and civil'. He attributed this state of affairs to the effect of the Church, who succeeded to the duty of 'correcting domestic immoralities which had been improperly entrusted to a civil officer'.

At the beginning of the nineteenth century the Church of Scotland stood at the height of its power, and it ruled with a rod of iron as a corrector of morals. Moral lapses were punished by making the offending parties stand before the congregation in church for up to fifty-two successive Sundays. Dr Edmondston saw the bad effects of this system when, in 1808, he described the ordeal of 'the fair, frail delinquents who for a single discovered imprudence, instead of being secretly reproved in the mild spirit of Christian gentleness . . . were indiscriminately stigmatized and repeatedly subjected to the sneers of a whole congregation'.

Records of the Kirk Sessions show how vigorously Sabbath observance was enforced. Some Foula men, noticing part of a wrecked ship drifting past the isle on a Sunday, launched their boat to secure it. They were hauled before the Kirk Session, but let off with a reprimand on condition that the money obtained from the sale of the timber should be handed over to the church to be used in connection with the work of the parish. Dr Hibbert describes the dilemma of a boat's crew engaged by him one Sunday on his visit to Unst in 1816. While off Uyea Isle a large seal came alongside the boat and the crew were distressed that the sanctity of the Sabbath prevented them from shooting it through the head. Then as the creature seemed reluctant to leave them one of the men became alarmed that perhaps it had come to welcome him to the depths for profaning the Sabbath. Of course it is not certain to what extent the boatmen were indulging in a little leg-pulling, for no doubt the islanders of those days were as adept at that practice as they are today. In any case, when they got to Haaf Grunay the sanctity of the Sabbath did not prevent each man leaving with as many seagulls' eggs as he could carry.

The 1820s were marked by a religious revival in Shetland, when Methodists, Baptists and Congregationalists all made inroads into the strength of the Established Church. Religious fervour affected all sectors of the community, and some of the best lay preachers were crofters and fishermen. Founder of Shetland Methodism was John Nicolson, who had served in the Royal Artillery during the Napoleonic Wars and who had become a Methodist in London. The first Baptist church in Shetland was established at Dunrossness by Sinclair Thomson, a crofter and fisherman who as a young man had experienced the rigours of several whaling seasons in the Arctic and before his conversion had had a profitable sideline as a pilot for a smuggling vessel that made regular trips to Shetland.

The Church of Scotland suffered another setback with the Disruption of 1843, when ministers broke away to form their own Free Church. In most cases they were followed by a large number of parishioners. Foremost in the movement in Shetland were Rev. James Ingram and his son, Rev. John Ingram, ministers in Unst. Out of a roll of about 1,300 members, no fewer than 1,054 followed them into the Free Kirk. Within a few months they had their own church at Hillside, Baltasound—the first Free Kirk to be opened in Shetland.

During the remainder of the century religion played a great part in the life of these islands, and visitors were often introduced to this aspect of life in Shetland long before they reached here. The artist, John Reid, visiting Shetland in 1867, tells of how the master of the schooner *Prince Consort* held nightly worship in his cabin, attended by all the crew except the man at the wheel.

Most people, however, carried their religion lightly, and it in no way lessened their zest for the typical island forms of amusement. On week nights dances and other functions continued to be held and the music of the fiddle was heard as loudly as ever, although some ministers did their best to suppress it. The Sabbath, however, was a day of sanctity. In many houses only the minimum of work was done on Sunday, while as many tasks as possible were completed on Saturday night, and before the family retired to bed all newspapers and books of a secular nature were put away.

In July 1894, at the monthly meeting of the Burgh Commissioners of Lerwick, concern was expressed at the activities of the steam yacht *Kate*, which was profaning the Sabbath day by taking passengers on trips through Lerwick harbour. Surprisingly, the steamers which plied between Lerwick and Aberdeen were exempt from censure, and dock workers often loaded and unloaded these vessels on Sundays when their schedule was upset by bad weather. The inter-island vessel *Earl of Zetland* frequently sailed for Unst on Sunday, but the Company found a neat device for camouflaging this fact. On their notices the sailing was billed as 'leaving from Lerwick every Saturday night or following day'.

It became fashionable to criticize the ministers of last century for their narrow-mindedness, their lack of humour and their severity in attempting to repress the natural gaiety of the people. In many cases the ministers of the Established Church were criticized for their apparent failure to condemn the many evils of the period—some were even accused of being in collusion with the lairds. But the ministers found it impossible to express their opinions freely since a laird could make life as difficult for the minister as he did for tenants.

Most ministers were dedicated men, many of whom spent their entire working lives in Shetland, giving comfort, advice and assistance to their parishioners and doing their best to improve living conditions. It must not be forgotten that many of the agricultural improvements of the nineteenth century were introduced by ministers of the Church of Scotland. Theirs was a hard job made more difficult by the scarcity of roads, which made visiting an ordeal. It was a life of virtual exile from their families and the way of life to which they had been accustomed in the south. They had little in common with their parishioners and could not even enjoy a meal with them, since the island diet of meat and fish, whether fresh, salted or sour, was not the food of the manse. It is not surprising that ministers relished the infrequent visits of other churchmen and dreamed of the day when their turn would come to attend the General Assembly of the Church of Scotland held each year in Edinburgh.

Towards the end of the nineteenth century a change became apparent with a growing awareness of the problems of Britain's farthest north. The question was discussed ever more frequently in the House of Commons, although several years were to elapse before the necessary legislation could be got through. The year 1879 saw the publication of one of the finest books ever written on these islands—Dr R. Cowie's *Shetland. Descriptive and Historical*, and this was followed in 1883 by John R. Tudor's *The Orkneys and Shetland*. These served to introduce to an interested British public what had been until then virtually a foreign country. An increasing number of visitors came north, captivated by all they saw—the scenery, wildlife, antiquities and the way of life of the people which, they realized, had not changed basically in hundreds of years.

The opening of the Queen's Hotel in 1864 and of the Grand Hotel in 1887—both of them in Lerwick—played a great part in encouraging tourism. Outside of Lerwick boarding houses were few and visitors had to depend on the hospitality of ordinary people. John Reid describes his visit to Foula in 1867 and relates how he was given the same menu for breakfast, lunch and tea—boiled eggs, oatcakes, flour scones and tea. The situation was the same in 1881 when Tudor visited the islands, and he advised visitors to Foula to carry a pocket enema to counteract the effects of a monotonous diet.

The new interest in Shetland was extended to the language of the people, their culture and their folklore. Shetland became the subject of numerous lectures and newspaper articles, many of them hopelessly inaccurate. The islanders had their own ideas about this influx of visitors, most of them polite and courteous, but some lordly and overbearing, and quite a few naïve and gullible. An old crofter in Foula was surprised to find a party of tourists making the best of a picnic in the wind-swept gref of a peat bank. He went home to enjoy his meal of fish and tatties beside a blazing peat fire, and he remarked to his wife that neither tinkers nor tourists had much idea about comfort.

3

The Dialect

During the long period of Norse rule Shetland had a language of its own as distinctive as Gaelic is today in the Hebrides. It was known as Norn—a branch of the West Scandinavian language then spoken in Norway, Iceland, Faroe, Shetland and Orkney. From the Scandinavian mother tongue there developed the independent languages: Norwegian, Icelandic and Faroese as we know them today, but in Shetland, as in Orkney, the natural evolution of the language was cut short under the growing influence of Scotland.

There was never any law passed to suppress the use of the old form of speech in Shetland, but, as happened elsewhere in Britain, the homely language of the local people was despised by the new arrivals who dominated the islands. Lowland Scots was the tongue of laird and minister and of the large number of Scottish settlers who arrived in the period following the transfer. Although in no way superior to the original inhabitants, and certainly no better educated, they were more likely to succeed in business or in whatever trade they followed because they spoke the same language as the laird. Naturally the local people were forced to conform, and for the old Norn language it was the beginning of the end.

In the more remote parts of these islands Norn lasted a surprisingly long time, for in 1593 when a new minister came to Unst it is related that he had to go to Norway first to learn Norwegian because none of his parishioners could understand any other language. For this reason he was known for the remainder of his ministry as Magnus Norsk. In other parts of the islands the dominance of the incomers was more quickly achieved. In 1631 an Englishman, John Smith, came to Shetland to assess the potential of the islands' fishing industry, and his subsequent report contains many points of interest quite apart from his information on the fishing industry. He states: 'The chief inhabitants of the island are Scots but the meaner or inferior sort are a mixture of Danes and Scots.' Less than 200 years after the transfer to Scotland the once proud udaller was a despised peasant in his own country.

One of the Norn verses that somehow survived remarkably intact comes from Unst, and refers to a young man going to Caithness and returning home full of the new Scottish words which could both please his superiors and impress his friends:

> Der vara gua ti
> When sono min guid to Kadanes.
> Han kan ca rossa mare
> Han kan ca big bere
> Han kan ca eld fire
> Han kan ca klovandi taings.

which translates roughly as follows:

> It was in a good hour
> That my son went to Caithness.
> He can call rossa mare,
> He can call big bere,
> He can call eld fire,
> He can call klovandi taings.

In a fascinating way this indicates the actual conversion of one Norn speaker to the Scottish ways, and in a similar way it must have been repeated all over the islands.

A feature of Norn that continued unadulterated for many years was the ballads or visecks sung as an accompaniment to old medieval dances similar to the ring dances of Faroe, in which a large number of people joined hands and danced in a ring. A leader would sing the verses while the others joined in singing the chorus. But inevitably these too declined in the early years of the eighteenth century as the people came to despise the old historical ballads and the ring dances were replaced by Scottish-type reels.

Norn lingered longest in the North Isles and in Foula, where in 1774 George Low met an old man, William Henry of Guttorm, who could recite a long poem in Norn, although he could only offer a general outline of its meaning. Mr Low recorded it phonetically and it was later identified as an old Norn ballad known as the Hildina Ballad—a tragic story of love and violence. It tells of how Hildina, daughter of the King of Norway, married an Earl of Orkney against the wishes of her father and in defiance of her Norwegian suitor Hiluge. It goes on to tell of how Hiluge slew the earl and compelled Hildina to return with him to Norway. During the wedding banquet Hildina extracted her revenge when after drugging the wine she set fire to the house as Hiluge and the guests slept.

In place of Norn there developed a dialect whose grammatical structure was basically Lowland Scots—itself an English dialect—but which was heavily interspersed with Norn words and phrases, while even the Scots words were given a distinctly Scandinavian pronunciation and accentuation. But inevitably the Norse element weakened steadily throughout the nineteenth century, one of the factors in its decline being the absence of a written language to provide a Norn literature. Had the Scriptures been translated into Norn the whole language might have survived, but sadly the only part of the Bible that could be recorded in Norn was the Lord's Prayer.

In the 1890s the dialect attracted the attention of Mr Jakob Jakobsen, the Faroese philologist, who between 1893 and 1895 travelled to all parts of the islands talking to people and listing the Norn words they used in everyday speech and, as important, the words they remembered their parents using. For the people of a small township gathered in a but end and recalling the old words and phrases it was a pleasant if unusual way of passing an evening. But to Mr. Jakobsen it was a methodical and time-consuming task. Some places were visited more than once, partly because his first visit had awakened such lively interest in the old language that people had begun to make notes and much more information had accumulated. After working for several years on this material, he assembled his findings in the form of a thesis for which the degree of Doctor of Philosophy was conferred on him by the University of Copenhagen.

In 1901 he published *Shetlandsøernes Stedhavne*, a treatise on Shetland's place names, published at Copenhagen, which sought for the first time to relate the thousands of such names to the old Norse language from which they had sprung. Nor was his study confined to the larger townships and major geographical factors—it was extended to every headland, every valley, every hill and hillock and even to the rocks under the sea. For Shetlanders, their place names suddenly took on a new meaning when they realized how apt most of them were.

Then followed the work for which he is best known, the four volumes of his monumental *Etymologisk Ordbog over det Norrøne Sprog pa Shetland*, also published at Copenhagen. Unfortunately he did not live to see the publication of the final volume of his life's work, for he died at Copenhagen on 13th August 1918, aged fifty-five. An eagerly-awaited English translation of the dictionary appeared in 1928.

Dr Jakobsen found more than 10,000 Norse words in the dialect rather more than half of which were still in common use at the end of the nineteenth century. The fact that so many old words had survived was to him an indication that it was not very many years since Norn had been a living language. He found that Norn had remained much closer to its parent Norwegian tongue than had Icelandic or Faroese, not merely because Shetland was much closer geographically but also because strong economic links had continued until the early nineteenth century. It is interesting to note that Dr Jakobsen was able to deduce from a comparision with Norwegian dialects that when Shetland had been colonized a thousand years earlier the vast bulk of the settlers had come from the South-west of Norway between Bergen and Mandal.

Dr Jakobsen came at a fortunate time, since at the end of the nineteenth century there still continued a way of life that had changed little from the time of the Norsemen. It was a life of crofting and fishing, of tilling the ground and rearing animals and practically everything they needed they had to make themselves. Hence there was a name for every part of the house, for every part of the boat and for every implement and utensil used in their working day.

A characteristic of Norn was precision, and there are hundreds of words for which no equivalent can be found in

English. The wool on a sheep had different names depending on which part of the fleece it was located. The folds of wool under the neck—reckoned to be the best wool of all—were known as the haslok, while the inferior wool growing on the belly was known as the aliplukkens. Great importance was attached to the physical appearance of the animals, and there were numerous words to describe different colours and combinations of colours. A gulmjoget cow was one with a dark body and a lighter breast and belly; a lendet cow had stripes of a distinctive colour across the loins, while a kappet cow had a dark body and a white streak running lengthwise along the back.

The list of adjectives applied to sheep was even longer. A katmoget sheep was one with a light-coloured body and darker underparts; a blaegit sheep was white with black spots; a bjelset sheep had a distinctive ring around its neck while the adjective mirk-faced was applied to a white sheep with brownish spots on its face. Many of these adjectives are still applied to sheep, as are the colours known as moorit or dark brown and the peculiar steel-grey colour known as shaela.

The vocabulary indicated an existence lived close to nature, utilizing the simple materials available yet developing a full and varied way of life. There was a great number of different types of baskets for carrying and storing various commodities. The large basket carried on one's back was known as a kishie, while a büddie was a fisherman's basket used for carrying home his catch. In Dunrossness a small meal basket was known as a loopi while in other parts of Shetland it was known as a kuddie or as a toyeg.

Dr Jakobsen was not surprised to find differences in the vocabulary from place to place. In most parts of Shetland a crø is a sheepfold, but in Unst a crø is an enclosure for growing cabbages from seed—a structure that is known as a crub in other parts of Shetland. This and other examples confirmed his contention that the original Norse settlers had come from different parts of South-West Norway, bringing with them their own dialects which influenced the form of speech in different parts of Shetland.

He was intrigued by the names given in different parts of Shetland to the wall that projects from the sheep fold to assist in the penning of sheep. In Unst it was known as a soadin daek (from old Norse *soeta* meaning to waylay); in Fetlar it was a rekster daek (from O.N. *rekster*, meaning the driving of animals) and in Yell it was known as a stillyers daek (from O.N. *stili* meaning a trap for animals). Even on the Mainland there was no uniformity, since in Northmavine it was known as a retta daek (from O.N. *rett* or sheep fold) while in Central Shetland it was a stuggi daek or crø stuggi, which Dr Jakobsen suggested might be derived from O.N. *stuka* or sleeve.

Many of Shetland's wild birds and animals are still called by their old Norse names, the otter being known as dratsi and the rabbit as kyunnin. A guillemot is known as a tystie, the Manx shearwater as a liri, while a seagull is a maa and its young are known as scories. Fish, too, have distinctive Norse-sounding names, a dogfish being known as a hoe while the tusk is a brismik and a ling, especially a young one, is known as an ollik. In several cases a single species may have four or five different names applied to it depending on its age. In this way a young coalfish or saithe is known as a sillock, but when two years old it becomes a piltock and at three years old it becomes a cüid while a stage between sillock and piltock is known as a steevin.

Some of the most beautiful of the dialect words are those connected with the sea. The name haaf, originally applied to the ocean itself, survives as a name for a deep-sea fishing ground, but *sjo*, the general Norse word for sea, had been lost by the time Dr Jakobsen carried out his research. Surprisingly he found it surviving in compound words such as shoormil— the strip between low and high water (literally the edge of the sea) which he regarded as an illustration of the dying of the old language. Broken water was known as hak; a sharp sea or tide lump was a burrik, while brim was the sound of the sea breaking on the rocks and brimasteuch the spume that hangs over an exposed stretch of coastline on a rough day.

One of the most beautiful words in the Shetland dialect is mareel (O.N. *mar ild*—literally sea fire)—the phosphorescence that appears occasionally due to the presence of tiny marine creatures. They may be seen at times adhering to the blade of an oar as it is raised for the next stroke, and they may be left for a few seconds on the gunwale of a boat that is being drenched with spray.

Again the many aspects of Shetland's climate have contributed a wealth of words to the dialect. Thick mist almost turning to rain is known as dag; a fivvel is a thin layer of snow, while snow falling in large flakes is known as flukkra. Here again the Norse obsession with exactness is evident, and in the gradation from light wind to hurricane there is a scale almost as precise as is the Beaufort scale. A pirr is an occasional light wind disturbing a summer's calm, and when the wind is more steady although still light it is known as a laar. A fresh wind is known as a stoor while a gooster is approximately the same as a strong wind, and above that there is a gyndagooster or storm. There are names, too for different types of wind. A guzzel is a dry, parching wind such as commonly blows from the southeast in the months of March and April, while a flan is a sudden squall that may come bearing down from the hills and which, by suddenly striking against the sail, can cause a boat to overturn.

Some of the most expressive of dialect words are those used to describe the sounds made by animals—the sneg and nikker of a horse, the reein of a pig, the yaarmin of a sheep, the nyir of a cat, the peesterin of a mouse and the klaag of a hen. Old people could listen to the sound made by a cow and discover whether or not it was in good health. The usual sound was a brül, whereas a gulbrül was an excited roar, a skrøl had an element of fear. A njoag was a nasal sound and a drund was a moaning sound indicating pain or discomfort. Merely by listening to their animals the people could in some cases diagnose the nature of the complaint.

Dr Jakobsen found a great variety of words to describe personal moods and behaviour. A person could be stutset, trumsket, trulshket, snoilket, snüsket or drøbi depending on the degree of one's sulkiness, while a person who was described as troinsket was one who made a trøni or long face. A person who moved wearily was described as drulset, one who walked slowly, almost reluctantly, was said to drittel, while someone in a hurry was said to 'geng wi a dirrel'.

While the Norse element is undeniable, the importance of the Scottish element in the dialect must not be overlooked. Many of the dialect words cherished so lovingly are actually archaic Scots words brought into the vocabulary by the incomers of 400 years ago. The dialect shares many words with modern Scots—words such as hame, hoose, bairn, moose, kirk and coo that come into both forms of speech from an older Norse tongue. Many of the Scots or English words incorporated in the dialect are modified in accordance with certain Shetlandic usages. A characteristic of the dialect is the persistent use of 'd' where the Scots or English equivalent is 'th'. Thus father, mother, weather and bother become faider, midder, wadder and budder, and of course 'the' becomes in the dialect 'da'. In some cases where 'th' occurs at the end of a word it is shortened in the dialect to 't'. Examples are hert for hearth, wirt for worth, cloot for cloth but the 'th' is retained in sooth and mooth. The ending 'ight' generally becomes 'icht' in the dialect as in licht, fricht and micht.

The grammar is essentially English but there are one or two exceptions. In the dialect the verb 'to be' is used instead of the auxiliary verb 'to have' in conjugating other verbs. The dialect equivalent of 'I have seen him' is 'I'm seen him', or 'he has come' is 'he is come', while instead of 'we have heard about it' a dialect speaker says 'We're heard aboot it'.

Another characteristic of the dialect is the frequent use of the pronoun 'du' in the second person singular. Although taken direct from Old Norse it follows all the archaic English forms of thou, thee, thy and thine while there remains a suggestion of an older Norse association in the form 'dis is dines'—'this is yours'.

English vowels are insufficient to cover all the vowel sounds of the dialect and it is necessary to retain the modified 'o' of the Norse language (written ø) which is sounded rather like the French 'eu'. Examples from the dialect are crø and trøni. There is also the modified 'u' written as 'ü' as in büddie and cüid.

Besides Norse and Scots words there are a few Dutch and German words derived during Shetland's long association with Continental merchants and fishermen. An older generation might have said 'kop' instead of 'buy' (cf. German *kaufen*) and 'rook' instead of 'smoke' (cf. German *rauchen*) while a small coin was for long known as a 'stoer' (cf. Dutch *stiver*). There are also French words that come presumably from the days when Shetland seamen languished in French prisons. The list includes 'vive' meaning 'bright' and 'bulyamints' meaning 'clothing' presumably from the French word 'habillements'.

It is not surprising that Dr Jakobsen found the Shetland dialect such a source of wonder and delight. While he bemoaned the loss of so many old words he regarded it almost miraculous that so many had survived the space of a thousand years. But even as he carried out his research he realized that yet another influence was at work—the influence of English following the introduction in 1872 of a compulsory system of education. Dr Jakobsen was far from optimistic when he wrote:

'This education in which the use of English is impressed upon the children and the use of such words and phrases as are peculiar to the Shetland dialect is not permitted in the schools will involve, in the near future, the Anglicizing of practically the whole speech.'

In this prediction he was to be proved wrong, for one of the most astonishing features of the dialect is its tenacity and its ability to survive in the face of apparently overwhelming odds. Had it been otherwise Dr Jakobsen would not have found the dialect such a fertile field for academic research.

RIDDLES AND PROVERBS

An attractive feature of Norn was the large number of guddiks or riddles, cleverly contrived and all of them pertaining to aspects of island life. Some of them survived until the nineteenth century and one or two of them, badly mutilated, were recorded by Dr Jakobsen.

Best preserved of these Norn guddiks comes from Unst:—

> Fira honga, fira gonga,
> fira staad upo skø;
> twa veestra vaig a bee
> and een comes atta driljandi.

The answer is 'a cow' and the translation can be rendered as follows:—

> Four hang (the teats) and four go (the legs)
> four stand skywards (horns and ears)
> two show the way to the town (eyes)
> and one comes shaking behind (tail).

As the Norn language lessened its hold the guddiks suffered a gradual translation into a dialect form, and where it was essential to preserve the rhyme Scots words were substituted. They remained a pleasing characteristic of the islands, being provided to amuse the family when sitting round the fire on a winter's night. The people showed considerable ingenuity in finding a puzzle in an ordinary feature of daily life and in the homely household articles dear to the heart of the family. Take this one:

> Tink tank, in a watery bank,
> Ten aboot four.

The answer is a woman milking a cow, the first two words being the sound made by the milk spurting into the pail while the last line refers to her ten fingers and thumbs gripping the four teats. Another well-loved riddle was

> I gaed oot atween twa wids
> An cam in atween twa waters.

The answer is a man going to the well with empty wooden buckets and returning with them full of water.

Easier and more readily identified by a younger child were these:

> I grew wi da coo yet wis made by a man,
> I böre till his moo whit boiled ida pan.

Answer: a horn spoon.

> Roond laek a millstane
> lugged laek a cat
> staandin upo tree legs
> Can du guess dat?

Answer: a kettle.

They found inspiration in nature and the changing moods of Shetland's climate.

> Bank fu an brae fu.
> If do wid gadder aa day
> Du widna gyet a nev fu.

Answer : mist.

> Fleein far but fedderless
> New come oot o Paradise
> Fleein ower da sea an laund,
> Deein in me haund.

Answer : snow.

> Lifts ower da hedder,
> Sinks ida sea,
> Fire canna burn it
> Whit can it be?

Answer : the sun.

> Hoopitie crookitie, rinnin me lane
> Cairdin oo aff a muckle stane,
> Whirmin among da heddercowes,
> Shaestin mesel roond da ferry knowes.

Answer : a stream.
Some had subtle undertones based on human behaviour.

> Whit is it at tears een anidder aa day
> An sleeps in een anidders' airms aa nicht?

Answer : Wool cards.
And perhaps the best loved of all guddiks is this one :

> I gaed oot ae mornin in May
> An fan a thing in a cole o hay.
> It wis nedder fish, flesh, fedder or bane
> Bit I keepit it till it could geng its lane.

Answer : an egg.
Still another attractive feature of the dialect handed down from Norse times is the large number of proverbs. There was a saying appropriate to every aspect of human behaviour which when uttered at an appropriate moment could not be bettered and indeed generally ended the conversation. When in a crowded household an older unmarried woman lost patience with

the children their mother might remark cuttingly: 'a yield soo wis never guid wi grices'. Inevitably young boys would get into trouble, especially when their pranks got out of hand, but an older person might console the mother with the words 'Mony a pellit (ragged) foal haes made a good horse'. And when it seemed that the family was having more than its share of trouble on account of the young people's waywardness, some-one would remind them 'Dere broken pots in aa laands' and instantly the situation was seen in its true perspective. At the same time a good upbringing was of paramount importance for 'It's late time to sift when da sids is ida bread'.

In every language love and marriage contribute a great many sayings, and the Shetland dialect is no exception. It was considered a bad sign when a romance started with too much ardour, and an appropriate saying was 'Cald is da kale at cøls ida plate an cald is da love at starts ower haet'. Again friendships that developed slowly were always the more durable, and should there be a sudden display of friendship between erstwhile strangers someone might remark: 'Dey'll hear o da pairtin at never heard o da meetin'.

A pretty girl anywhere is soon married, and in Shetland the appropriate saying was 'a bonny bride is shün buskit'. But a girl left on the shelf could console herself with the thought: 'Better lang lowse dan ill teddered'. Should two people with obvious shortcomings decide to get married someone was bound to remark: 'Hairy butter is good enyoch for siddy bread'. And in this proverb there is all the sorrow of a jilted girl keeping her grief to herself—'Better ee hert braks dan aa da wirld winders'.

The Shetlanders were good judges of character, and in this category there are dozens of proverbs such as 'da lazy man is shün forbidden'. The equivalent of the pot calling the kettle black was 'Hit's ill for da kettle crook tae ca da kettle black'. Of a frivolous person it could be said: 'Caff (chaff) aye flees heicher dan guid coarn'.

They learned from experience never to take things at face value and never to imagine that a new laird, merchant or minister would be better than his predecessor—'Better da ill kent as da guid untried'. And no matter how attractive a new policy or new idea might appear they advocated caution with the

words: 'Dere few rodds at doesna hae a mire at da end o him'.
Caution was expressed in the saying 'never hüve oot dirty
water till da clean be in'.

In a close-knit community it was important to keep on good
terms with one's neighbours, and many sayings express this
sentiment.—'A freend ida wye is better dan a penny ida
pocket'; or 'Hit's no lost at freends get' and: 'Ye can win by aa
yer kin, bit by yer neebir ye canna win'. They realized the
damage that gossip can do in the expressions: 'Da lesser said
da süner mended' and: 'Ill news is laek a fitless heddercowe'—
it went flying like a clump of heather without a root.

The hard work shared by men and women alike gave rise to
numerous proverbs such as 'Every man's back is shapit for his
ain burden' and 'Da back haes mony an ill day for da belly'.
But there was no use sitting idly wishing for one's lot to
improve—'Glowerin ida lum never filled da pot' and 'Dey'll
no ploo muckle at coonts da nails ida ploo'. Thrift was essential, for 'A penny hained (saved) is a penny gained', and they
learned to make do with very little—'A moothfu is as guid as
a belly fu', or 'better lang little as shüne nane', and 'better a
half egg dan an empty skurm (shell)'. At the same time they
realized that when food or money came after a time of scarcity
it went all the faster: 'Lang want is nae maet hainin'.

Among the host of proverbs and wise sayings, perhaps the
most appropriate of all and one that can almost be taken as
the motto of the crofter-fisherman is: 'Da riven sleeve hauds
de haund back'. For the lack of a few pounds in ready cash he
was unable to take advantage of an improved type of husbandry or to invest in an improved fishing vessel. Instead he
had to carry on as his father had done before him, taking one
step at a time. The Shetlander was ever anxious about the
future, but no good could come from worrying about it.
Instead he took one day at a time with the thought: 'It's a guid
day at pits aff da nicht'.

4

The Croft

At the very heart of life in Shetland was the croft—a plain stone cottage and a few acres of arable land in the narrow strip of green between the hills and the sea. Crofting has been defined as a form of subsistence agriculture suited to the relatively harsh conditions of the North of Scotland. But this description does not tell the whole story—the croft was a foothold on the land from which the family could exploit every facet of their environment in order to survive. The croft by itself could not provide sustenance but by adding the resources of the hills and of the sea a modest kind of living was possible.

Crofting is a tradition with its roots in the distant past when the first Norse settlers broke out their garths and toons from the virgin hillsides. The early farms were merely patches of cultivated land surrounded by a wall or stockade and outside of these were setters or areas of grassland where cattle could graze in summer. But gradually as the population grew the pressure on the land increased and before long the setters too were put under the plough and spade.

By the end of the Norse period all the best land was under cultivation—a pattern of crofting townships occupying the inland valleys and the lower slopes of the hills. Each township, or room, was a group of perhaps ten or more crofts enclosed by a hill dyke that separated the arable land and improved pasture from the unimproved wastes of the hills. The hill dykes were never straight—they curved upwards from the seashore to where the hillside steepened, then they meandered as a rampart of stones and turf surmounted by a stockade of sticks before sweeping down to meet the sea again at the far side of the township. Usually the foreshore served as the lower boundary of the township and indeed it came to be considered as a valuable adjunct to the croft as a source of shellfish, seaweed, driftwood, and winter grazing for sheep and ponies.

The land within the hill dykes was divided into grades of quality, the best land, that tilled every year, being known as the infield. It was divided by balks or ditches into long narrow strips known as rigs, counting perhaps eight or ten patches to the acre. But the term 'acre' is a comparatively recent innovation. The old unit of measurement throughout much of the Scottish period was the merk—an indefinite quantity depending on productivity, whereby a merk of poor land might be double the area of a merk of good land which was in fact usually a little less than an acre.

Originally the land within the hilldykes was held under a complicated system known as run rig or rigga rendal. The system is now imperfectly understood, yet it was once common throughout Scotland and parts of Europe. It fell into disuse in the mid-nineteenth century but in a few parts of Shetland it lingered into the twentieth century and even now it is not quite extinct. It was a system designed to ensure absolute equality with each crofter having a share of the good land and of the poor, and the main drawback was that a crofter's land was scattered throughout the entire township. To add to the confusion in some districts the system of rotating run rig was held, whereby the individual patches were cultivated by each family in the township in strict rotation.

The poorer arable land was known as the outfield and it too was divided under the run rig system into little patches usually smaller than the infield rigs. The division was not absolutely rigid since through careful cultivation patches of outfield could be brought into an infield condition.

Although infield and outfield together occupied only a small proportion of the crofting land all of the land within the hilldyke played a vital role in the complex cycle of the crofting year. Around the house lay a small portion of land outwith the run rig system known as the toonmails and usually extending to about half an acre of ground. This included the site of the house itself, the yard and the kailyard, and the green slopes and knowes around the house where the milking cows were

tethered for part of the year. Where the crofts were close together the toonmails were contiguous and often formed a continuous strip running through the township separating the
houses from the fields below.

Where a stream wandered through a township the banks on
either side were generally too wet for cultivation, but valuable
nonetheless for the production of meadow hay which was an
extremely important commodity especially before the introduction of fodder crops. The meadows too were subject to the
principle of run rig but there was a great deal of variation from
place to place. In some places the meadow was divided by
imaginary lines into segments allocated to the various crofts
and sometimes worked in rotation. In other places hay was
worked 'in halvers' and subsequently divided among the part-
ners when it was cured.

The rest of the land within the hilldykes consisted of rough
grazing land or outrun, originally little better than the
heather clad hills outside the hilldyke, but becoming green
from continual cropping and from being fertilized by the dung
of grazing animals. Here and there were patches of better grass
which could be cut and cured as hay. Again these patches were
usually worked in one of the variants of the run rig system.

Beyond the hilldykes lay the common, a wide expanse of
hill and moorland where the animals of the township grazed
for most of the year. Until the middle of the nineteenth century the hills were undivided, being without fence or dry stone
wall, but each township or group of townships had its own
portion known as the scattald, bound by imaginary lines
known as the hagra. At points along the hagra were visible
marks known as hagmets—sometimes a pile of stones or a
naturally occurring earthfast boulder, while at other places a
pit or a trench might be excavated. Between Bretta and Sand-
water there is a hill known as Hagrafield and on its summit is
a pit set about with stones and known to the present day as the
Waal o' Hagrafield.

If inside the hilldykes the land was carefully tended outside
the boundary the opposite was the case. The hills were plun-
dered for earth and peat mould and even little patches of green
turf were uprooted and carried home to enrich the already
over rich soil of the infield. Until this practice was abolished

by statute many acres of moorland were stripped to bedrock
and carried home to be mixed with more usual types of manure. This undoubted carelessness was one of the points seized
on by the lairds in the late nineteenth century as an excuse for
dispossessing the people of what had been theirs for more than
a thousand years.

There was a second valuable source of pasture—the holms
and skerries that fringe the shores made green by the drop-
pings of seabirds. Wherever an islet was large enough to support a sheep or two in summer it was utilized and the larger
islets such as Colsay or Haaf Gruney were used to graze cattle.
One of the best examples of a holm being used for pasture is
the Sheep Craig at Fair Isle which the islanders climb with the
aid of chains and raise and lower their animals by ropes. On
top of the stack is ten acres of pasture and it is said that the
wind is deflected upwards by the steepness of the sides. Some
of the holms were held by the crofters in rotation and some
of them are still regulated under this system.

Although the township was not operated on a co-operative
basis as we know it today, the run rig system was an expression of the extreme co-operation that once marked Shetland
society, when people realized that every task was done better,
with greater ease and with more enjoyment when done with
the help of others, whether it be rowing a boat, spinning wool,
or cultivating a piece of ground. It belonged to a period when
people literally pulled together and when the lives of individuals were subject to that of the community as a whole. But in
an age when the importance of the individual began to assert
itself the run rig system was an anachronism.

Division of run rig actually began in the late eighteenth century and it continued throughout the following decades. The
process was speeded up in the mid-nineteenth century when
land became more valuable in the eyes of the lairds. Where
two or more lairds had an interest in a township it became
imperative to find out where each proprietor's limits lay and to
establish boundary walls and fences where none had ever exist-
ed before. Next the laird could apply the latest methods of
farming to his estate and either evict his tenants for sheep or
force improved methods of husbandry. Gradually the land
within the hilldykes was divided among the various crofters as

fairly as possible and before the end of the century most of the crofts were separate entities, many of them wholly enclosed with a wire fence.

There was great diversity in Shetland's crofting system at the end of the nineteenth century. Some crofts had been planked, some were still intermingled with neighbouring crofts under the run rig system and others had been cleared to make sheep-runs and the Cheviot and the Blackface had replaced men and women. But crofting was entering a new phase in which security of tenure had removed the constant fear of eviction; and the knowledge that improvements to a croft made by a family during their period of tenure would be rewarded should they vacate it had given an added incentive to improve their land and buildings.

CROPS

From the time of the Norsemen to the very end of the nineteenth century the most important grain crop was bere or four-rowed barley. It was always grown on the best land and given the lion's share of the manure. The other grain crop was oats, generally the old black variety, short in the straw, which was usually sown on the poorer outfield land.

Potatoes were introduced about 1730 and they soon came to be regarded as the most reliable crop of all. They were especially suited to the unpredictable climate of Shetland, being less prone to damage during the storms of late autumn. The people came to depend too much on the potato and when the crop failed extreme hardship resulted.

Another important crop was cabbage—the old Shetland variety with the bluish green leaves—sown in late summer in round, high-walled stone enclosures known as plantie crubs, and transplanted into the kailyard the following April. They were ready for use in late autumn and throughout the winter they remained a valuable supply of food for both humans and livestock.

The crofting mode of husbandry was frequently criticized by visiting agriculturists who failed to understand the peculiar problems of these islands. Many districts followed a five-year system of crop rotation starting with a ley or fallow period followed by oats for two years in succession, then a crop of potatoes succeeded by one of bere. The ley period especially came in for criticism, for instead of a crop of grass or turnips as was the practice on the Scottish mainland it produced only ragweed, mayweed and ox-eye daisies which went to seed, so that oats sown the following year had to compete with a profusion of wild flowers. In some places, however, even this simple form of rotation was unknown, and according to Henry Evershed there were places where bere was grown on the same infield plot year after year without either a period of fallow or a change of seed.

On the outfield the system was generally oats in alternate years with a fallow in between. When growing oats the manure was not applied until after the seed was sown, when both were harrowed into the earth together; but in the case of bere the ground was first dunged and the manure turned down before sowing. When grain followed a crop of potatoes the soil was not turned over. After sowing the seed the manure was spread on top and harrowed in with the seed.

There were numerous attempts to improve the situation and a great part was played by the parish ministers. In the *Old Statistical Account* the minister for Fetlar describes how Polish, Blindsley and early barley had been tried with success although they seldom ripened to perfection, being easily damaged by the equinoctial gales. The ministers also did their best to encourage the growing of turnips as fodder. Sown grass was unknown at the end of the eighteenth century, but the Rev. John Mill noted that on sandy ground protected from the cattle natural crops of clover and rye grass sprang as richly as on the sown fields of other parts of the U.K.

The Shetland Agricultural Society did a great deal to encourage crofters to sow grass and turnips giving premiums for the best crops. In the Society's second annual report in 1816 it was noted that almost every farmer in Tingwall was growing turnips and in Northmavine all Mr Gifford's tenants were doing so. In Tingwall some crofters had experimented with sown grasses, but since stock from neighbouring crofts had free access during winter the experiment was not generally followed. Indeed it was not until the run rig system was abandoned that the cultivation of these crops became general.

But in spite of these scattered attempts at improved methods of husbandry many crofters clung to the old ways, and as late as 1889 when the Crofters' Commission began their investigations there were witnesses who maintained that rotation of crops was impracticable.

LIVESTOCK

When the Norsemen settled in Shetland in the ninth century they brought with them their own cattle, sheep, ponies, pigs and poultry, and in each of these cases there evolved a typically Shetland breed, some of which continue to the present day.

Most important of the crofter's livestock were his cattle, which were regarded as only slightly less important than the people themselves. The Shetland cow is a small fine-boned animal with short legs, short slender horns, and a sleek, glossy coat usually black and white in colour, although a brown or reddish colour is occasionally found. Although small they are surprisingly good milkers, producing five to eight quarts of milk a day. It is a breed suited to a rather bare country such as Shetland, and it has been found that little improvement in size can be made even with better feeding either within or outwith Shetland.

A great affection developed between the people and their cattle. They responded to kindness and had their own favourites among the owners, as had the people among their animals. A cow could be stubborn and refuse to yield milk to a person other than the one she was accustomed to have milking her. 'Every byre has its leader', the people used to say, and sure enough in every byre there was one animal that seemed to dominate the rest, to dictate the mood that would prevail at a certain time and the response to a new situation. They were given descriptive names such as Blackie and Sholma, the latter from the adjective sholmet, used to describe a black cow with a white face.

During summer the young animals were allowed to roam loose over the scattald while the milking cows were tethered on the green knowes around the house. Then in winter they were confined in the byre, being kept alive on an inadequate diet of hay, straw, cabbages and, latterly, turnips. The byre was rarely cleaned out, the dung usually being scattered throughout the byre and covered with peat mould, dried grass or heather to absorb moisture. Alternate layers of dung and bedding accumulated until there was hardly sufficient room to stand. When this stage was reached in spring the rich mixture was carried out as manure for the infield.

When spring came the animals were frequently so weak from their inadequate diet that once having laid down they were unable to get to their feet again. This persisted even when put out to graze the new grass and the condition might last from January to May. It was described as being 'in lifting'.

As in the case of Shetland cattle, the progenitors of Shetland sheep were brought from Norway, and over the years there evolved a small race of sheep with an extremely fine wool. But the fineness of the wool was not fully appreciated, and no attempt was made to improve the breed nor even to keep it pure. In the *Old Statistical Account* Rev. John Mill tells of an English scabbed ram being brought into Dunrossness about 1790 and causing the spread of the disease throughout the parish until there were fewer than 5,000 sheep left south of Cunningsburgh. It must have been about this time that the great sheep dyke was built across the Clift Hills to prevent the northwards spread of the disease. It was maintained by the crofters of Cunningsburgh and played an important role in the containment of the outbreak.

It was only at the end of the eighteenth century that a serious attempt was made to safeguard the quality of Shetland wool by paying strict attention to breeding. The committee of the Highland Society of Scotland awarded premiums for the best specimens of the breed which they insisted should be kept separate to prevent adulteration.

At that time much of the islands' clip was virtually wasted in the knitting of coarse woollen stockings which sold for a nominal price of five pence a pair but were in reality bartered for tea, snuff, tobacco, linen and cotton. During the next thirty or forty years a change took place, for in the *New Statistical Account* the minister of Tingwall maintained that since new markets were found, particularly in England, the increase in value was nearly equal to the rent of the islands. And the improvement he ascribed to the patriotic and benevolent exertions of Sir John Sinclair.

Until recent times Shetland sheep were never clipped. At the appropriate time each summer the old wool loosens and can be gently pulled off by hand—a process known as rooing. Rooing has two advantages over clipping—it gets the whole length of the wool, which is important when the wool is naturally short, and it does not remove any of the new wool which is coming up below the old.

Although the animals belonging to several crofters grazed together on the scattald, each man knew his own animals, since, in common with other parts of Britain where the Norse have left their impact, each owner had his own distinctive mark—a hole, a shear, a crook, a rit, a fedder, a shüll or a combination of these cut into the ears of his sheep. Each mark of ownership was carefully recorded, as it is today, in a book kept by each parish. If anyone purchased a sheep from another man a special oobregd (off-break) mark had to be used to obliterate the original mark.

Until late in the nineteenth century there was no regulation of the scattald—each crofter could graze as many sheep as he wished, and some had as many as 200 sheep while others had only two or three ewes. Furthermore, attempts to improve the breed had been abandoned—inferior lambs were not castrated and the best lambs were often taken off and sold because they fetched a slightly higher price. But following the Crofters Acts attempts were made to regulate affairs on the scattalds. In the 1890s rules were introduced making dipping compulsory each year as a means of combating scab, lice and ticks. Before this, sheep were simply smeared with grease in a half-hearted attempt to prevent disease. In 1911 another act set up grazings committees to keep a strict control on the running of the scattald. In most cases an attempt was made to organize the numbers of sheep kept, each crofter being allocated a share of the total known as the 'souming'. But regulation was neither universal nor enforced. The Ward of Scousburgh, for example, was not regulated until 1963.

The Shetland pony is another example of a breed adapting to its environment, its smallness and its thick coat being products of the Shetland climate. Ponies were common in Norse times, as is proved by the prevalence of the word *hestr*, being incorporated in such place names as Hestamires, Hestensetter, and many more.

The colours of a Shetland pony are extremely varied and include black, dark brown, light grey, chestnut and combinations of these. The size too is variable, some standing as much as 11.2 hands high (forty-five inches) while the average is approximately nine hands high or about about thirty-six inches. Each crofter had at least one pony used for carrying loads and as a mount, while those crofters who lived at a distance from the peat hill owned four or five which were used to carry home the year's supply of peats.

The Shetland pony is at his best in late summer when his old coat has finally gone and his coat is sleek and glossy. In May, however, a different animal is seen, with his coat of the previous winter hanging in tatters—a stage in which he is known as a pellet rül.

Pigs are now seldom seen in Shetland, yet at one time practically every croft kept one or two sows and their young were reared on scraps of food and boiled fish heads, while small potatoes were reserved for them, and indeed are still referred to as 'grice mites' by older people. The Shetland pig was a small long-nosed animal with a short coat of thick hair, kept in a specially built sty or in an improvised compartment in the byre. During the summer they roamed the scattald, varying their diet with young birds and occasionally a newly-born lamb. By all accounts they were a detestable breed and were a menace to growing crops, as they exploited every weak point in the hill defences to gain an entry to the township. Hibbert described the Shetland pig as 'a little ugly brindled monster, the very epitome of the wild boar'. It had, however—one redeeming grace—it made excellent pork.

Poultry were far more important than they are nowadays. Flocks of geese were kept on the scattald during summer, ducks frequented the nearest burn, loch or shun and hens roosted in the byre, which they entered through openings in the roof just above the wallhead. They were given free range over the croft and greens, worms and insects accounted for a large proportion of their diet, but they were usually fed morning and evening with a small amount of meal or grain. The small Shetland hen was a terror in the fields in spring, and at one time it was common to have their feet smocked or sewn up in rags at seed time. The gander, too, often had a wooden clog on his foot, partly to prevent him getting among the fields of grain but mainly to prevent him taking to the air, since if this happened it was extremely unlikely that he or his protégées would ever be seen again. The practice of keeping geese declined in the last years of the twentieth century, and it was noticed in some districts that the decline in the number of geese coincided with an increase in the incidence of liver fluke among sheep. The suggestion was put forward that the geese had actually kept in check the numbers of the snails on which the liver fluke depend in one stage of their life cycle.

Crofts were usually overstocked. A typical holding of five or six acres might have two cows, their calves, yearlings and two-year olds, two or three ponies, two sows, thirty to forty ewes, two dozen hens and a cockerel, twelve ducks and a drake and twelve geese and a gander. Each year a young cow would be sold at the spring or autumn sales; eggs would be bartered at the shop for groceries, while before Christmas there was usually a fairly good demand for geese and ducks.

But income was of secondary importance, the main purpose of the croft being to render the family as nearly self-sufficient as it was possible to be, with their own eggs, their own meat, their own milk and their own wool. There was no such thing as specialization on a Shetland croft.

AGRICULTURAL IMPLEMENTS

The essential implement was the spade, which consisted of a stout wooden handle four feet long and an iron blade oval in shape measuring ten inches long by six inches broad. Immediately above the blade a projecting bar of wood served as a step to drive the spade into the earth.

A few of the larger crofts had ploughs—simple wooden devices entirely home made and so light that a man could carry them. The beam was a stout piece of wood bent naturally almost into the shape of a rectangle and tapering to the point where it was attached to the team of animals. The coulter or knife stood vertically and was too short to be really effective. A square hole was cut through the lower end of the beam to hold the mercal, a piece of oak just under two feet long which held the metal tipped sock and sky. The furrow was made deep or shallow by driving in a wedge either below or above the mercal as required.

There was only one stilt, or handle, to guide the plough and the ploughman walked, not behind it as in the case of later double-stilted ploughs, but at the side of it on the 'white' or unploughed land. It was an extremely inefficient implement, easily broken against a stone or by a stiff furrow. It turned the soil almost right over and people were employed to cut and smooth the earth with spades.

The normal ploughing team consisted of four oxen walking abreast. A large yoke was laid on the necks of the two outermost animals and a smaller yoke across the necks of the inner pair. The yokes were joined by a double rope to the middle of which was fixed a chain or draught which was from eighteen to twenty-four feet long and was fastened to the nose of the plough. Besides the ploughman and the workers who smoothed the earth, a driver was employed to lead the team, 'dragging the team after him' in the words of one eye-witness.

Ploughs were more common at the end of the eighteenth century than at the end of the nineteenth. In the *Old Statistical Account* the minister of Northmavine states that there were twenty-six ploughs in his parish but that the numbers were decreasing each year. It was claimed that the subdivision of the crofts under the pressures of a rising population resulted in smaller crofts which could be tilled quite easily by spade. The number of wooden ploughs decreased steadily throughout the nineteenth century, and when Henry Evershed visited Shetland in 1873 cultivation by spade was universal.

The other traditional implements were as simple as were the plough and spade. The harrow consisted of two parallel pieces of wood about four feet long with eight or ten wooden teeth in each piece, connected at the ends by cross bars two feet long. It was drawn by a man or woman by means of a rope tied to each end of one of the long sides. The loop was taken over the shoulder, then with his hands behind his back the operator grasped the ropes, leaned forward and walked over the ground two or three times until the seed was covered and the clods of earth broken up.

The Shetland scythe and sickle were also small and inefficient, although adequate for the scale of agriculture as practised. The former was simply a long pole with a short blade enabling the mower to stand erect while he worked. The Scottish scythe had a longer blade and cut a wider swathe and it displaced the old Shetland scythe in the latter half of the nineteenth century. The sickle or corn hook survived much longer and even now is not entirely extinct.

Other improvements came steadily throughout the nineteenth century. Even in the 1790s horses were employed in parts of Dunrossness and the lairds had Scottish swing ploughs on their home farms. But the crofters were slow in copying the example of the lairds. They had so little capital on which to operate, and the small acreage they tilled did not merit more sophisticated horse-drawn machinery. Nevertheless, by the end of the nineteenth century improved ploughs drawn by Highland or Icelandic ponies were common on larger crofts, especially in the more fertile parish of Dunrossness. Even here oxen were still in use, and a large acreage was tilled by the spade.

BUILDINGS

The Shetland croft complex showed little variation in design from the time of the Norsemen until the end of the nineteenth century. It consisted basically of three main compartments— a living-room and a bedroom for the family and a room for the cattle, all under one roof, entry being made through the byre.

A great deal of care was taken to make the byre as comfortable as possible, since the cattle played such an important role in the operation of the croft. Along one wall was a raised portion known as the bizzie separated by partitions into stalls where the cattle were housed. At the head of each stall a veggl or wooden stake was driven into the stone wall to serve as a fastener for the cow's halter. Behind the open ends of the stalls and running the length of the byre was a channel known as the runnik which drained away the urine through a hole in the end wall of the byre. One of the stalls usually served as a store for the peat mould that was used for bedding, and at the far end of the building was a loose box for calves. The byre also served as a hen house, having perches fitted over the runnik, while lay boxes and baskets were suspended from the rafters.

The barn was an important part of every croft and it was often built behind the main building with a connecting door through the shared wall reached by a passage between the byre and the dewlling-house. It also had an outer door leading into the yard where the grain was stacked. An essential component of every barn was a threshing floor, often comprised of planks of wood, where the grain was threshed with a flail, and on the wall hung the straw mat known as the flaakie, on which grain was winnowed to remove the chaff. A steady wind was essential for the winnowing process and a position between the two open doors of the barn was ideal for the operation.

The grain had to be dried before milling, and this was carried out in a kiln which occupied one corner of the barn. The kiln was a rectangular compartment about six feet long by three feet broad supporting lathes of wood known as kiln sticks. These were covered with a layer of straw upon which the grain was spread for drying. A fire was lit in the kiln huggie at the open end of the kiln, the smoke passing along the kiln and escaping through a flue in the back wall. The fire required constant watching, since if it burned too strongly the layer of straw could catch alight and the grain would be destroyed.

In the parish of Dunrossness the kiln was built as an appendage to the barn, a structure round in cross section narrowing towards the top and bottom to increase the draught. The kiln had a door about four feet up from the barn floor and at this height a ledge ran right round the inner wall of the kiln. In this type of kiln the wooden sticks were placed from the ledge to the kiln simmer—a piece of wood that ran across the middle of the kiln. From the bottom of the kiln a tunnel ran back into the barn and at its end was the kiln huggie where the fire was lit.

An indispensable feature of every barn was the quern or handmill, standing on a rough table known as a looder. The quern was used for grinding small amounts of grain, and whenever the water mills were not working, as during periods of drought or spells of frosty weather. It was also used to produce a delicacy known as burstane from bere dried in a kettle over the fire.

These compartments were basic to every croft, and in addition there was a great variety of smaller sheds and outhouses, some of them built simply from turf for storing potatoes, dry peat mould and other commodities. There was frequently a pigsty and a house for ducks and geese, while a large lamb house was essential for housing the lambs during their first winter. An old fishing boat hauled ashore and turned upside down could be made into a very desirable shed for livestock. It only required a low wall with a door, for when lifted into position it provided both the upper half of the walls and the roof. In crofts where a work pony was kept a stable was essential and this frequently took the form of an extra compartment in the croft complex. But unlike the byre and the barn it was never interconnected with the house.

The Crofting Year

The crofting cycle began in the depths of winter, as gales lashed the islands and heavy seas pounded the coast casting up piles of seaweed on exposed beaches. This was a crop that never failed and one that was extremely important to the crofter, for when rotted it made excellent manure. In the short, dark days of winter men and women alike were busy piling the seaweed in mounds above the high-water mark—'laying up waar' they called it. During a lull in the storm it was loaded into kishies, carried up the steep path from the beach, and dumped in huge waar middens which were left to decompose until voar by which time they were ready to be spread over the rigs.

Winters are long in Shetland, the hillsides grey and the low-lying fields sodden from the perpetual lashing of rain. But towards the end of March a change becomes apparent as an easterly wind, cold off the North Sea, starts to dry the surface of the land. Then slowly the transformation begins as the first signs of growth cause a faint green shadow to darken the hillsides, and for sheep and cattle alike 'da green paek' brings a welcome relief from the privations of winter.

As it remains today, one of the surest signs of voar was the burning of the heather, the white smoke scenting the air and the crescents of flame spreading stealthily against the wind. Heather burning was strictly controlled and an old Act of Parliament decreed that the operation should be carried out

A typical late nineteenth-century croft

Shetland breed of cattle

Cutting oats with a corn hook

An old-style wedding

House interior

Cutting peats with a tushkar

Using ponies to carry peats in the island of Fetlar

A peat carrier, knitting as she walks

Water mills at Huxter

Making a straw kishie

Herring fleet leaving Lerwick in the 1890s

A steam drifter discharging her catch

Sixerns at Fedeland

before 11th April, by which date moorland birds were usually preparing to nest.

By early April voar work was underway in earnest and the whole township showed signs of the new awakening. The hill dykes were carefully repaired, the grinds were hung and the livestock banished to the scattald where they would remain during the next six months. Only the milking cows were allowed to remain within the township but restricted by tethers to keep them off the fields.

Most of the land was turned over by the spade by men and women working in groups of three standing shoulder to shoulder, moving from right to left across the rig and working from the bottom towards the top. In this way after many years earth accumulated at the foot of the rig while the top became denuded, but from time to time earth would be carried to the top in kishies to even things out.

They worked as a team digging over the earth in unison. The iron blades were placed about a foot from the edge of the unturned portion of the rig, then each of the team lifted his or her right foot and pressed down on the heel of the spade. The long clod of earth was carefully prised loose, lifted an inch or two and turned right over. All day long the field echoed to the ring of iron against stone and the clash of spade against spade as they broke the lumps of earth and chopped the upturned roots of grass and weeds. A row was called a geng, and when it was completed the trio would usually stop and straighten their back and talk or joke for a few minutes before walking back to start another geng.

It was tiresome work made more difficult by the earth and manure clogging their spades and sticking to their boots. The working day was long, starting after breakfast and interrupted only for dinner and tea before ending about eight p.m. Nevertheless it was satisfying to smell the new earth and to see the darker area eating up the grey as the work progressed.

When setting potatoes the seed was first of all cut at home and carried to the rig in a kishie. When a geng was completed one of the three, generally a woman, would take a pail, fill it from the kishie and set a row of seed in the furrow, cut face downwards and spaced about the length of her shoe apart. Then the earth from the next geng would cover the seed.

Oats were sown in April, scattered broadcast from a seed kishie slung in front of the sower. While conditions were right for germination sowing became a matter of urgency. 'A day in voar is a week in hairst' the old folk used to say. Traditionally all the oats had to be in the ground before Simmermill Day, 25th April according to the old style. Bere, on the other hand, was not sown until May.

With the seed in the ground the men turned their attention to the peat cutting, and as May progressed the lambing season demanded the attention of the entire family. It was a constant scouring of the hills seeking for weakened lambs and driving off swaabies and ravens. Throughout the nineteenth century the erne or white-tailed eagle—a species now locally extinct— was another pest especially destructive at lambing time. Early in May the haaf fishing season began. The men of the house went to sea, and from then until early in August the work of the croft was left to the women, the children and the old folk.

The lambing over, the family could again turn their attention to the crops. The potatoes had to be hoed and earthed up and the neeps had to be sown and singled, but for the grain crops there was little to be done and the people could wait and watch. It was said to be a sign of an early harvest if the bere was 'shooting' at Johnsmas—24th June. Invariably the rigs became infested with runchie, a yellow weed that gives out a sickly smell after rain. The leather jacket, or story wirm as it was known, was a pest over which the people had little control, and it was believed that the only remedy was to let the ducks eradicate the pest, which they did most effectively, working over the infected patch until all the grubs were removed.

Summer in Shetland is a few months of paradise. The meadows are thick with wild flowers, red and white clover brighten the roadside and large ox-eye daisies sparkle in the fields of grain. There is no darkness at midsummer but the 'simmer dim', a kind of twilight, falls at midnight. Through the summer months the peats required constant attention as they steadily accumulated in larger piles. The sheep had to be caaed or driven several times for dipping, for rooing, for marking the lambs and finally for weaning the lambs from their mothers and separating those to be sold or slaughtered from those to be 'set on'.

On the day chosen for caaing all the people of the district

would assemble with their dogs. Each person knew his own duties beforehand, some them having to go to the very limits of the scattald perhaps five or six miles away. Gradually, with much shouting, barking of dogs and bleating of sheep they would converge on the crø, long lines of sheep merging into streams and finally coalescing into rivers of white, flecked with brown and grey, as they neared the pen where they would be guided through the entrance and the gate shut. Inevitably one or two would try to be awkward and make a dash for freedom only to be headed off by dogs and people. But the crø was far more than a place of work—it was a meeting place where people could exchange news with neighbours on the other side of the hill.

It was essential to roo the sheep at the correct time, when the old wool was loosening and ready to be pulled off. But some animals shed part of their fleece before caaing and it stuck in tufts to heather and barbed wire. These hentilagets were considered public property, and many a poor old woman with no sheep of her own gathered sufficient wool to make herself a set of warm underclothes for the winter.

The first of the crops to become ready was the hay, mown in the meadows in August, the swathes being turned when dry and built into coles. When thoroughly dried it was carried home in meshies—pannier-like open baskets made from well-laid straw simmonds, and latterly from old meal bags or strips of canvas. In the yard the hay was built into a dess or stack, rectangular in cross section, tapering upwards towards the top. It was built on a foundation of stones, dry heather and grass and was tied securely against the winds.

The first of the potato crop was also ready in August. It was too early to lift the plants but by purling or poking with the fingers underneath the tubers large enough for use could be removed and the others left to grow undisturbed. The first meal of new potatoes with their strong, earthy taste, was one of the highlights of summer.

August was a crucial month as summer merged into hairst. A sudden storm could do untold damage, and the people did not like to see the potato flowers shaken off by the wind. A heavier crop was expected when the flowers were allowed to wither naturally and ripen into potato 'apples' hanging in dark green clumps. Another threat to the potatoes came from blight that thrives in warm, muggy conditions. When the white daala mist lies thick in the valleys it is a sign that conditions favour the spread of the disease. It is not surprising that people used to believe that daala mist was the cause of blight.

In August the men returned from the haaf stations in time for the crucial weeks of the year. Oats and bere were generally ready in September, and sometimes when a storm was expected they would be cut when only partially ripe, otherwise they might be flattened by the rain and twisted by the wind. On those occasions the scythe was of no use and the people had to revert to the corn hook. The greatest danger of all came in late autumn, when a gale could shake off the grain, leaving the straw as clean as though it had been threshed.

Even in good seasons harvesting was a laborious job—shearing by scythe or corn hook, henting or gathering the stalks into a bundle and binding the sheaf with a band of straw prepared by knotting two handfuls of stalks together. But gradually the job was completed and the yellow fields gave way to rows of stooks drying in the wind. Then came the final moment of victory when the sheaves were carried home and built in a skroo in the yard beside the dess of hay.

Carrying in the corn was known as hirding, and when it was all safely in the yard it was said to be gorhirded—a word that reflects the triumph of the occasion. It was also yarfasted— tied securely to the ground with especially strong home-made ropes or simmonds known as gorsimmonds or yarsimmonds.

The final crop to be harvested was the potatoes and this was not done until the leaves had blackened and fallen off and the shaws had turned white, when the tubers would leave the dead plant of their own accord. They were generally riped or gathered in October and either pitted in the ground or stored in a shed or a special potato crø in the byre or barn. Heavy rain in low-lying rigs could delay harvesting until November while early frost could ruin part of the crop. No part of the harvest was completed without the danger of failure. And hairst was crucial to the family's very existence—it was a gathering home of food to withstand in reasonable comfort a long cold winter.

There remained one final task—almost a ceremony to be

performed to mark the end of harvest. When all the crops were safely in the yards of the township the grinds in the hill dykes were taken down and every man's sheep, cattle, swine and poultry were allowed to roam in perfect freedom over the entire township, picking whatever grass remained on the fields and along the stanks and gorsties. This was known as the right of ockrigert or the custom of slipping the ockrigert. This was part of the principle of equality involved in the run rig system to ensure equal shares for everyone. It was especially beneficial for the poor, giving their cattle a chance to gain strength for the long cold winter.

Shetland winters are long and dreary, a succession of gales and long periods of rain. For weeks at a time outside work was impossible, but there was plenty for the crofter to do indoors. The oats were threshed to separate the grain from the straw, then the ears were winnowed to remove the chaff. Before milling the grain had to be dried in the kiln while in the case of bere the grain had to be hummelled—put into a tub and pounded with a shovel to loosen the anns or remains of the beards before being made ready for grinding in the quern or in the water mill.

Winter was hard on the animals. For the cattle in the byre feeding was a scanty diet of straw and hay, cabbages and turnips. Even the cabbage stalks were split lengthwise to expose the soft pith so that nothing but the hard outer skin was wasted. Sometimes the cows were given hinniwirs from the seashore to eke out their diet.

The lambs wintered in the lamb house, fed daily with hay, potatoes and cabbage cut up small. But for the older sheep there was no such favoured treatment. They had to shelter from rain and blizzard in the lee of a stone wall or in the dubious shelter of a peat bank where they were frequently buried under drifting snow. They could survive a surprisingly long time, remaining alive by eating the wool off each other's backs. For much of the winter when the ground was frozen their only source of food was seaweed, and when the tide began to ebb lines of sheep could be seen making for the beach.

Even with the coming of the New Year there is little improvement in the weather. There is a saying that 'as the day lengthens so the cold strengthens', and it is true that the coldest weather usually comes in January and February. The 17th day of January used to be called St Anthony's Day or Antinsmass, and this day was believed to coincide with the start of a spell of exceptionally cold weather. 'Da snaw never comes intae da hoosis till Antinsmass', they used to say, and again: 'Antinsmass snaw is da warst snaw'. But just as in the death of the old year the new one is born, so in the heart of winter the new crofting cycle had already begun.

5

House and Home

House building techniques showed little variation from one end of Shetland to the other. The walls were fashioned from two skins of stone, trussed together at frequent intervals with trowbaands or larger stones that stretched the full width of the wall. The space within the wall was filled with clay or earth as building proceeded.

At the aesins or wallhead, flat stones known as aesin flags were placed with their upper surfaces tilted slightly outwards to divert the rain water and prevent it soaking into the heart of the wall. But when house and barn shared a wall this arrangement was impossible, and the rain water ran down to meet in the angle formed between the two roofs and percolate down through the rubble. This was a design fault which was never overcome, and during wet weather the back wall of the house was constantly damp.

The roof consisted of couples resting on the wallhead strengthened halfway up by horizontal bars known as twart baaks that ran across the house. The couples were consolidated in the other direction by long, thin lathes of wood known as lang baands, placed more or less regularly on top of the couples in a horizontal position. Next came lengths of hedder sim-monds—ropes twisted from heather and chosen for their long-lasting quality as well as for their roughness, which helped to prevent the subsequent roofing material from slipping.

The first of the roofing layers was a covering of poans—thin slabs of turf fixed to the couples and to the lang baands by wooden pins. They were placed rather like slates with the lower edge of each row overlapping the upper edge of the one below, while the ridge was finished off with a layer of poans folded to hang down on either side and again fastened by wooden pins. In some areas there is found a special type of vegetation consisting of moss and heather roots growing in shallow soil on top of hard rock or stony clay, and this can be torn off in long strips. Such strips were known as flaas and when available they were regarded as superior to poans.

A large amount of thatching straw, or gloy, as it was usually called, was used as the upper covering for the roof. The bundles of carefully selected straw were spread out to a uniform thickness on top of the poans, each row of straw overlapping slightly the one below. They were held down by simmonds of straw stretched tightly from gable to gable and again fastened to the poans with wooden pegs. Finally the ridge was covered with bundles of straw folded in the middle to hang down on either side and spread out to produce the required thickness. When the herring industry grew in importance cotton nets, when no longer fit for use at sea, were cut into sections and laid on top of the thatch to keep it in place. But netting was not essential since the entire roof covering was tied down by long ropes of straw spaced about fifteen inches apart known as da links and weighted down on either side of the roof by heavy link stanes, resting on the thatch about a foot above the wallhead.

In the oldest type of house there was no outer door. Entry was made through the byre which served as a kind of porch to shelter the door of the house itself. A typical dwelling-house measured thirty feet long by twelve feet wide and the side walls were about five and a half feet high rising to high peaked gables that ensured a steep slope to the roof. It was divided into two compartments—a but end, or living-room, and a ben end, or main bedroom, the former being about twice as large as the other. In most parts of Shetland the floors of both rooms were of trodden clay, but in Dunrossness the but end was often floored with flagstones.

The but end itself was divided into two by the hearth or hert stane placed midway between the front and back walls and rather more than half way in from the door to give a larger 'ootby' part of the floor as a working space and an inner 'inby' space used rather like a sitting-room. The hert stane was actually composed of several flat stones embedded in the floor, the spaces being filled with clay. One slab stood higher than the others and this was the backstane against which the fire was banked.

The dividing wall between the two rooms was generally a wooden partition, but in smaller houses the division was formed by a box bed standing with one end against the back wall, or by two box beds standing in line, in which case the gap between the beds served as the entrance to the ben end.

The earliest houses had neither windows nor chimneys but three large openings or lums high up on the roof, two of them above the but end one above the ben end, which served the dual purpose of letting out smoke and letting in light. The lum was protected on the outside by an inclined board known as a skyle, and whenever the wind changed direction it was necessary to rotate the board so that the opening faced away from the wind. This was done by means of a pole from inside the house and the operation was known as 'skylin da lum'.

From the reports of visitors it is clear that there was considerable variation in house styles. According to Dr Hibbert, writing in 1817, the best houses in Shetland were those around Quendale where some even had slate roofs, proper windows and chimneys and detached byres. In other places the houses were far less elaborate and some had only a low partition of turf to separate but and ben while refinements such as windows and chimneys were found only in the houses of ministers and lairds, although some croft houses no doubt had small gligs or skylights in the roof.

In the latter half of the nineteenth century a considerable number of minor improvements were made. Following the repeal of the window tax small windows became quite common, but even as late as 1873 Henry Evershed wrote of seeing narrow slits to let in light, closed with bladders or lambs' skins more often than with glass. In some houses the fireplace was moved to an end wall and a proper chimney helped to overcome the problem of smoke. Another improvement was made by taking out a door on the front wall of the house and blocking up the door between house and byre. In those cases the but end was still divided into ootby and inby, the latter being the end nearest to the gable. Although earthen floors continued in most houses a few of them were provided with a raised wooden platform to provide a degree of comfort at the inby end of the room.

Although built from simple materials, there was a definite grace about the old Shetland croft house. It was as rugged as the rocky hillsides from which the stones were quarried and it blended with the countryside in a way that no house does today. There was little attempt at decoration since in those days survival was the main aim in life and luxury and embellishments were practically unknown. There was no flower-garden but there was a yard where the crops were stacked in autumn and usually one would find honeysuckle and red and white roses growing in the shelter of the wall. There were few trees apart from the widdie (elder) which was commonly grown as a windbreak although it too required the shelter of a dry stone wall. As in the case of so many other refinements proper gardens were the preserve of the clergy and of the gentlemen who lived in mansion houses at Baltasound, Tresta, Sound and other places.

The croft house had no lavatory, but privacy could always be found in the byre when weather or home commitments prevented one from seeking a secluded spot outside. The proximity of the midden below the outfall from the byre was another inconvenience since the area in front of the house was frequently little better than a quagmire. Dr Hibbert described the stepping stones placed in front of many houses 'to prevent a plunge knee-deep into the immense bed of compost that lay all around'.

In spite of these obvious inadequacies it was remarkable that from such simple materials there could be built a house that offered a surprising amount of comfort. It was low to lessen wind resistance and even during winter gales it was a surprisingly silent house with no slates to rattle and no casements to clash. It was, above all, a warm house in winter and a cool house in summer since the thick walls and heavy layer of thatch were excellent insulating material. The main requirement that had to be met was that it must be built as cheaply as possible considering the relative poverty of the people. In fact the Shetland croft house cost next to nothing to build—

only a great deal of time, and in those days time was not equated with money.

FURNITURE

The fireplace was the heart of the house in more ways than one. In older houses a stout log of wood known as the crook baak stretched the full length of the but end supported by the front and back walls and placed directly over the fire. From this was suspended a heavy iron chain known as the links which was provided with an S-shaped piece of iron known as the crooks, upon which the iron pots were hung, and which could be set at the desired height above the fire depending on the size of the pot and the amount of heat required. Peat smoke filled the room, swirling in the draught above the heads of the occupants and escaping eventually through the openings in the roof. Yet even the smoke was not wasted, since in combination with the heat from the fire it fulfilled an important function. The space under the roof was known as the reest and was used for curing a variety of meat and fish and for drying such commodities as cabbage seeds, hides and bundles of floss. Lathes of wood and strips of simmond netting laid across the twart baaks supported the heavier articles, while others were draped over ropes known as raeps stretched across the room.

Another feature of every croft house was a large shelf or laim extending the full width of the room and supported on a pair of joists placed about three feet apart. The laim could be placed at either end of the but room and it served for storing crofting implements such as ropes, baskets and nets, in fact anything that had to be stored in a dry place rather than in the byre or in an outshed.

Another essential article of furniture was the restin chair—a kind of sofa made of wood and entirely uncushioned, usually six feet long with arm rests at each end. This was the best chair reserved for guests and senior members of the family, while the others had to make do with simple wooden chairs and the children sat round the fire on stools or creepies. There was also a wooden table used during the preparation of food and at meal times, but it could rarely accommodate the entire family. It was perfectly in order to take one's plate or bowl to the restin chair, while the children usually sat on stools with their bowls resting on their laps.

There were numerous chests, large and small, for storing clothes, and their lids also served as seats or even tables at times. There was usually a box for holding peats—the peat-lodi —and near the door a water benk or bench consisting of battens supported on stones. Here stood the wooden daffiks or buckets in which water was carried from the well. Other essential articles of furniture were a tall press or cupboard for holding kitchen utensils and a rack for holding crockery.

The traditional Shetland lamp was the kollie—a simple device made by the local blacksmith. It consisted basically of two iron shells, the upper acting as the reservoir for fish oil with a projecting spout in which lay the wick. The lower shell acted as a tray to catch oil dripping from the wick. The lower shell and the upright back of the kollie were made in one piece, the back being bent forward at the top and terminating in a spike or sometimes a hook. The upper receptacle was a detachable vessel usually smaller than the other and attached to the main part of the lamp on a notched bar that projected in a slight incline forwards from the back. The wick was the pith of a dried stalk of floss lying in the spout of the upper shell, and as the oil was consumed the level at the wick was restored by tilting the reservoir—moving it along the projecting bar one notch at a time.

The kollie was either stuck into a roof beam, suspended from a cord, or hung upon a raep that traversed the centre of the room from end to end. In the latter case it could be moved easily to wherever light was required. It gave but a poor light, and as the liver oil burned it gave out a sickening smell. But the great advantage of this type of fuel was its abundance and its cheapness.

In the ben end the box beds occupied a large amount of floor space. As the name suggests, they were large wooden boxes about six feet six inches long and four feet wide, raised about one foot off the floor on four wooden legs that extended upwards to form the main framework of the bed. The entrance to the bed occupied about one third of the front side and this could be closed by wooden doors. There were no door knobs, but a hole in each door allowed one's fingers to gain a grip and they also served as ventilators. In some cases the holes were carved in ornamental shapes such as hearts or diamonds.

It is not known when box beds were introduced, although it seems that they were common by the beginning of the nineteenth century. Nevertheless Dr Hibbert gives the impression that in 1816 only better class croft houses had them, and that in many cases the beds were little more than bundles of straw in any convenient corner of the house, but as well as ben. By the end of the nineteenth century the box beds were an essential part of most croft houses, but already iron bedsteads and home-made wooden ones had made their appearance.

At first the ben end was simply furnished with two or three box beds, a wooden armchair, the meal girnal and odds and ends overflowing from the but end. It was lit either by a kollie or by a tallow candle stuck, perhaps, in the neck of a Dutch krook. But an improvement took place towards the end of the nineteenth century. As in the case of the but end, a proper window was taken out in the front wall and wooden sleepers were laid down on the earthen floor and covered with planks to make it more than merely a bedroom. With a table on which lay the family Bible and a peat fire blazing in the gable, it became for the first time the best room, fit for the entertainment of special guests such as the minister or the laird's man when he came to collect the rent.

Improvements came in other aspects too. The old kollie lamp was replaced as early as the 1860s by lamps that burned paraffin. The earliest ones, shaped like coffee pots, were made by tinkers. Then came the glass fountain single wick lamps which were almost universal as late as the 1920s, being followed in turn by lamps fitted with incandescent mantles. And in both but and ben mantelpieces above the fire served as a receptacle for ornaments such as china dogs brought home by seafaring members of the family, and invariably a handsome American clock ticked the hours away. The inner walls were whitewashed, and after successive applications much of the roughness of the stone face was camouflaged. Framed family portraits and calendars from the local shop were hung on the wall. But however important, those improvements did not affect the basic shape and plan of the croft house, which remained unaltered in some places until the early years of the twentieth century.

DOMESTIC UTENSILS

Few of the articles used in the home were purchased—most of them were made by the people themselves just as the earliest inhabitants of Shetland had done in prehistoric times. Indeed a relic of the Stone Age persisted until the late nineteenth century in the shape of the knockin stane—a large lump of freestone hollowed out in the centre—in which small amounts of bere could be shelled by being pounded with a stone mell or mallet.

The quern was another ancient implement—a handmill consisting of two circular stones similar to the type of mill introduced to Britain by the Romans. Grain was fed with one hand through the eye in the top while the other hand turned the upper wheel by means of a projecting handle. The quern was still in use in the early years of the twentieth century.

Wood was used in a great number of ways, being fashioned into pails, tubs, cogs and kits, into shappin trees and gruel trees, egg cups and tall wooden churns. A high-hooped vessel for holding milk to be churned was known as a span, while a wooden tub-shaped vessel for holding run milk was known as a remikel. In Unst a wooden vessel broader at the bottom than at the top and designed for holding oil was known as an oili hoilk, while in Dunrossness a similar vessel was known as an oili roobel.

Sheepskins with the wool removed were stretched over wooden hoops and pierced with straightened-out fish hooks made red hot in the fire to produce sieves of different fineness —the grof sieve and the fine sieve—while a similar implement unpierced and known as da blinnd sieve or in the North Isles as da weits was indispensable in cleaning meal after grinding. Numerous containers were required for storing meal, salt and other commodities. These could be made of wood or straw, while a sheepskin sewn into a buggie made a useful container for a variety of commodities including wool and meal.

Only around the fireplace were implements of iron essential. The cooking pots, the large black kettle and the teapot were purchased from the local shop while the tongs, the griddle and the brand iron were made by the local blacksmith and when treated carefully would last a lifetime.

Earthenware jars and dishes have been in use for centuries imported from the Continent and latterly from Britain. China cups and plates assumed greater importance towards the end of the nineteenth century being proudly displayed in a laem rack. Horn spoons were made by the people themselves, being shaped in a special wooden clamp or mould known in some places as da clams. By the end of the nineteenth century manufactured articles began to replace most of the home-made articles, but some articles such as churns remained in use for several decades longer.

FOOD

A large part of the working life of both men and women was spent in the production of food. It was not taken for granted as it is nowadays and there was constant anxiety that the family might go short, especially as sowing time approached when most of the remaining potatoes, oats and bere had to be set aside for seed. In the best years food was barely sufficient and in poor seasons large amounts had to be imported from Scotland, while in exceptionally bad years considerable quantities of meal and potatoes were provided by charitable bodies such as the Society of Friends. Visitors were often surprised to discover that the opening topic of conversation when meeting local people was the price of meal at Leith. It was assumed that this question would be uppermost in the minds of visitors too.

Oatmeal and beremeal were used in an incredible number of ways to impart variety to what would otherwise have been a monotonous diet. They were baked into scones and bannocks, brünies and krüls; they were made into porridge or gruel and a special type of gruel made with milk instead of water was known as mill gruel.

During milling the grain was ground into meal of varying fineness which was separated by the sieves. Even the sids or husks were not wasted. They were 'set' with water in a little wooden span and allowed to stand for a week to produce the sharp, refreshing drink known as swats. The remaining solids when strained through a cloth contained all the remaining nutrients of the grain and it was cooked to make the delicious food known as soins. Yet another grain product was burstane produced when bere was dried in a kettle over the fire and ground in the quern. It was baked into brünies or eaten with hot mik in the dish known as pramm.

Potatoes played a large part in the traditional diet figuring prominently in the main meal of the day. In addition tattie bannocks were considered a delicacy, especially if dusted with fine oatmeal before being cut into rounds and baked on the griddle. Cabbage became important in winter in such dishes as lang kail, short kail, kail and knockit coarn and tartanpurry. In the latter dish the liquid in which the cabbage had been boiled was kept overnight and used for making the porridge next morning.

Milk was plentiful and churning took place at least once a week. As in the case of grain, the products of the churn were diverse, as the people used their ingenuity to extract the last grain of value from the milk. When the butter was removed boiling water was poured into the buttermilk. The remaining solids then separated to form kirn milk, a kind of soft cheese, while the remaining acid but pleasant-tasting liquid, known as blaand, was the most common beverage in Shetland if we exclude tea. Ale was seldom made on account of the scarcity of grain, although it was common in the eighteenth century, and in 1817 Dr Hibbert tasted 'native ale' at Fogrigarth near West Burrafirth.

The first milk from a cow after calving was known as beest. It had a peculiar rather strong taste and was used in its own range of recipes. Beest pudding was made from beest baked until set firm and flavoured with salt, cinnamon and carroway seeds.

In spite of certain inadequacies the traditional Shetland diet was far richer in protein than that of the ordinary people in most parts of Britain. Meat was plentiful in the latter part of the year. The first lambs were slaughtered at Lammas followed by rams at Michaelmas and hogs at Hallowmas while the best hog of all was reserved for killing at Yule. There was a great mistrust of undercooked meat, since it was believed that a disease once common in Shetland and improperly called leprosy was caused by eating underdone food; hence there was a tendency to boil meat far too long. Nevertheless all the nutritional value of the meat was concentrated in a pot of mutton broth or kail soup.

No part of the sheep was wasted, even the haarns or brains, the neers (kidneys) and lichts (lungs) being utilized while the head became the basis of a nourishing broth. An old verse recited to amuse a child runs as follows:

> Dance dance dizzy fit
> Whistle Tammy Young
> Sheep's head athin de pot
> An du sall gyit de tongue.

A sheep's tongue was a delicacy not encountered every day.

Sheeps' entrails were used for making puddings, and each part had its own name, such as the Muckle Bag, the King's Head and the Lackie. Some of the intestines—the sma puddens —were also utilized, while the final section of the large intestine of both sheep and cattle was used for making sparls. The scraps of meat, especially the fatty parts and gristle off the breast and foreshoulders were minced together, seasoned with salt and pepper and stuffed into the tube which was then sewn up and laid in a tub, sprinkled with salt and left overnight. Next morning the sparls were wiped clean with a cloth to remove the slime and hung up in the roof to dry. They became ready after three to four weeks hanging in the peat smoke and would keep good for several months.

Inevitably there was a surplus of meat when the animals were slaughtered in the autumn and a dearth of fresh meat during eight months of the years. Some means had to be devised for preserving food and the answer was found in drying. At one time every household had a skeo or roughly built stone hut with plenty of spaces to let the wind through. Mutton dried by this mean was known as vivda. In 1774 George Low found hundreds of them in use and he commented rather unfavourably on the smell. Gradually the skeos fell into disuse throughout the nineteenth century and latterly they were used for drying fish. Now the word 'skeo' is remembered only in place names such as Skeotaing in Unst.

This practice was displaced by the process of light salting before drying. Shoulders and legs of mutton were steeped in

pickle for three or four days, then hung in the reest and allowed to dry until they became as hard as bone. Slices or portions
were cut off as required and boiled with cabbage in soup. The
flavour was excellent. Beef was usually salted down in a barrel
where it would keep in a solution of salt, or salt and sugar, for
up to nine months.

Fortunately for Shetland there was a year round supply of
fresh food that came from the sea. The waters around these
islands teemed with fish, for the problem of overfishing had not
begun to make its mark. There was a great number of different
species including herring, mackerel, haddock, whiting, ling,
cod, tusk, skate, halibut and many more. Even when the
weather was too stormy to allow the men to go after these deep
water species, young saithe or coalfish, known locally as sillocks and piltocks, frequented the voes right up to the rocks
where they could be caught by rod and line and taken in large
quantities by pock or dip net. In certain years when the crops
failed the people were kept alive for months at a time on a diet
of piltocks. Patrick Neill described how in September 1804 he
inquired of a crofter what he had for breakfast and the answer
was: 'Piltocks.' What did he have for lunch? The crofter
replied 'Piltocks and cabbage'. What about supper? Again the
answer was: 'Piltocks.'

As in the case of meat nothing was wasted. The livers of
many species were considered a delicacy and made into dishes
such as stap, gree'd fish, liver heads, liver muggies, krampies,
krappin, mooguilden, haka muggies and slot. In Dunrossness a
favourite dish was liver cüides when piltocks with their livers
left inside them were roasted on the fire. Livers and fish oil
played such a great part in the traditional diet of the Shetlanders that several visitors claimed that this element in their
diet gave them immunity from many diseases.

Fish too were dried during periods of plenty and kept in
reserve for periods of bad weather in winter. The amount of
salt used in their cure dictated how long the fish would keep
and also determined its flavour when cooked. In the early part
of the nineteenth century fish were dried unsalted in skeos to
produce blawn fish but the practice ceased with the abandon-
ment of the skeos. Nevertheless partly dried unsalted fish remained popular. Skate was often hung up on the gable of the

house and kept until partially sour when it was considered a delicacy in spite of the strong smell of ammonia that accompanied the eating of it. Cod heads dried on the walls of the houses formed the staple diet of the poorer people in certain parts of Shetland during the cod fishing season. Some species were heaped in the open for a process known as 'soornin', while whitings lightly salted and partially dried in the sun were known as sookit whitings and had a delicate flavour all of their own.

Most of the fish, however, were thoroughly salted to enable them to keep for a year or more. Herring were salted in barrels while ling, cod, tusk and saithe were soaked in pickle for a few days then spread out to dry until they became as hard as wood. The commercial catch was exported to Spain and Ireland while a small amount—generally that caught outwith the normal fishing season—was cured by the family for their own use.

There were other sources of food obtainable at different times of the year, including the eggs of seabirds in early summer, while the young of several species were eaten in many parts of Shetland. Dr Hibbert tells of how the people of Gloup in North Yell let down hooks on lines over the cliffs and jerked them upwards to catch young birds. The people of Foula derived a great part of their food from the seabirds that nested in the cliff ledges there, but it was a dangerous practice and many men lost their lives. Shellfish such as whelks and spoots were collected on the beaches and the type of seaweed known as hinniwirs was used occasionally. Taking everything into consideration there was great variety in the traditional diet of the Shetlanders but it was not constant and the most important items were undoubtedly fish and potatoes.

THE DAILY ROUND

Considering the varied duties of the family there could be no such thing as a typical day. To a great extent the working hours were determined by the season, and in summer the family were astir soon after six o'clock, while in the winter there was less urgency and mornings being dark few people were awake before eight. For those engaged in fishing there could be no hard and fast rule, since some of the branches of the fishing industry entailed working at night and snatching a few hours'

sleep during the day. Again in most parts of Shetland the summer fishing, whether by line or drift net, involved staying away
from home between Monday and Saturday from May to
August.

Invariably the first duty of the earliest riser was to stir the
fire, clear away the ashes and add fresh peats to the glowing
embers. Then the kettle would be hung in the crooks to boil
water for the morning cup of tea. While someone prepared the
pot of gruel for breakfast the men would attend to the cows in
the byre and give each of them a few handfuls of hay or a hallo
of straw, then the women would milk them before sitting down
with the other members of the family for the first meal of the
day. In summer the cows had to be not only milked but also
tethered on the pasture before the women could have breakfast.

Thereafter each set about his own duties. For men the work
was generally out of doors—in the rigs, at the peat hill or at
sea—while the women had their own household duties in addition to the demands of the croft. There was a constant coming
and going throughout the day, carrying in peats and water,
flitting the cows, milking them for the second time at noon,
perhaps putting them outside the hilldykes for the afternoon
and bringing them home at night. In addition there was churning to be done, clothes to be washed in the wooden sae, bread to
be baked and a dinner of fish and potatoes to be prepared then set
on the brigstanes to cool. In summer time outside work went
on until eight or nine at night interrupted only by tea at five
or six.

In winter it was different, since outside work came to an end
in mid afternoon and during the remainder of the evening the
whole family was busy round the fire. While the women sat
carding and spinning their wool and knitting gloves, socks,
haps or spencers, the men were busy mending nets and lines,
making kishies, winding simmonds and repairing boots and
shoes. Even the children were not idle—the boys were busy
cutting kail for the lambs' morning feed and learning from
their elders the skills they too would some day have to put into
practice. Girls had a harder lot than boys, since it was unseemly
for a girl to be seen 'sitting hand idle'. A motto engrained into
the minds of girls from an early age was: 'Lass tak dy sock.'

As the people worked they chatted oblivious to the weather

outside. Work would be laid aside for a cup of tea at eight o'clock after which the children would be pushed off to their beds which were usually warmed with large round beach stones first heated near the fire then wrapped in an insulating cover of brown paper and cloth both to keep in the heat and protect the toes from being burned. Thereafter work was resumed in the but end, the pace becoming more and more desultory as the evening wore on until banter and laughter predominated while the air became thick with tobacco smoke mingling with the peat reek overhead.

Even before the coming of clocks and watches the people had a keen sense of the passage of the hours. In summer the sun was an excellent timepiece while in the winter time was noted by the position of the stars—especially 'da seevin starns' (Pleiedes) and 'da leddy ell waand' (the three stars of Orion's belt) but it was said that the stars 'raved' after Yule. A far more reliable winter timepiece was the moon, and when it stood above a prominent landmark the people could tell the time with amazing accuracy even though this varied from night to night during its various phases. As in so many other fields the Shetlanders of a bygone age were far more conscious of the revolution of the planets than are their descendants today.

Supper was a pot of fish and potatoes or perhaps a pan of mill gruel set on the table and everyone dipped into it with their spoons. Then the fire was rested—its glow partly extinguished by having ash heaped over it—and after laying their outer clothes over a chair or a chest the people entered their box beds and the doors were drawn shut. One box bed was reserved for the daughters of the family and one for the sons, while the parents had a bed to themselves, sharing it with the youngest child until he was old enough to join his brothers and sisters in the appropriate bed.

While the winter storm raged outside the crofter and his family, his cattle and his poultry slept snuggly in their respective compartments. At certain times of the year cats and dogs might share their sleeping quarters with an ailing lamb, a piglet, or even a calf which soon felt quite at home in the but end.

It was a picture of peace, as the firelight flickered and cast long shadows on the pots and pans, the chairs and chests, the spades and sillock pocks, trout nets and lambs' tethers and many other articles required by the family in their varied duties by land and sea, all gathered around them in the but end.

It was a hard life but a comparatively happy one far removed from the pressures of international affairs. Intruders from the outside world came now and then when ships were wrecked on the rocks, and of course Shetlanders were always at sea somewhere, frequently fighting in other peoples' wars. It was a life in which money played a trivial part, the greatest worry being that they might be unable to raise the five pounds or so to pay the annual rent. And coupled with this was the constant fear that they might be turned out of their house at the whim of the landlord—a fear that was finally removed with the passing of the Crofters Act in 1886. Only one thing was certain—the strength and loyalty of the family. This was an asset which helped to compensate for the undoubted hardships of Shetland crofting life.

6

Special Skills

Before the days of regular all-the-year-round communication with the Scottish mainland the people of Shetland had to. be virtually self-sufficient and they developed a versatility that never failed to surprise visitors to these islands. In 1895 Dr James Bryden summed up the position when he wrote in a newspaper article following a visit to Foula: 'They make their own turning lathes, looms, spinning wheels, cloth, clothes, boots, shoes, clogs, furniture of all sorts, boats, spades, mills, wheelbarrows, in fact everything they need'.

The islands had few natural resources, yet what they had was utilized in a surprising number of ways. Stone was the universal building material, generally rough and difficult to cleave except in the coastal strip between Lerwick and Dunrossness, where sandstone has for centuries provided excellent building material. Elsewhere schist and gneiss had to suffice, while in some parts of the mainland the blue-grey limestone was commonly used.

Limestone served another purpose, since it was burned in specially constructed kilns to produce lime for building and for agricultural purposes. One of the oldest kilns was that at Fladdabister which was mentioned by Dr Hibbert in 1817 as producing lime for the town of Lerwick.

Relics of the Stone Age lasted a long time in Shetland with such articles as querns and knockin stanes surviving in use to the end of the nineteenth century. Kleber or soapstone, being soft and easily worked, was put to a variety of uses being carved into sinkers for fishing lines, whorls for spindles and weights for looms. Stone was also used for making the moulds required by blacksmiths when shaping kollie lamps.

What the islands lacked in the way of home-grown timber the beaches made up with an abundance of driftwood. Deals from passing ships and even the timbers of wrecked ships themselves were sawn into couples and lang baands and fashioned into chairs, restin chairs, dressers and household utensils. There developed an amazing skill with wood and there was no need even for the art of the potter, since after being soaked in water to swell the kits, cogs, tubs and barrels were as watertight as any glass bottle or earthenware jar.

Such was the variety of wood the people could afford to be selective. Pitchpine was best for the handles of spades, tushkars and other implements; ash was best for the handles of hammers and chisels; oak was essential for the stem of a fishing boat, while silver birch was used for pirns and other parts of a spinning wheel. Indeed in some parts of Shetland birch was known simply as pirm wid.

Nothing produced on the croft was wasted. Skins of animals killed or found dead were made into leather, and well into the nineteenth century the roots of tormentil—a little yellow flower that grows among the heather—were used in tanning. Slippers known as rivlins were made of cowhide or sealskin while the skins of sheep were most valuable of all. After being limed to remove the wool the skins were cured and tanned to be made into skinjoups worn at sea. Sheepskin was also used in the making of skinbows (buoys) as were dogs' skins and calfskins and occasionally their stomachs.

In most districts the only specialist was the blacksmith who made the iron parts for spades and forks, and the axles for wheelbarrows and spinning wheels. But the people could use their skill with wood to lessen their dependence on iron. Instead of metal door hinges, the door of the house pivoted on a wooden pin—the sharl pin—rotating in a wooden socket known as the haar, while the sneck or door latch was simply a short bar of wood pivoted to allow it to be lifted over a wooden keeper.

The ingenuity of the Shetlander was seen even when travelling in foreign lands, since time and again his eyes alighted on a piece of wood or other material that had a direct application to life back home. An extremely functional case for knitting needles could be made from a section of bamboo closed at the bottom by a natural joint while the other joint formed the lid.

Even the common apparently worthless plants that grew around the croft were used in a variety of ways. Baskets were made from straw, floss or dockens, ropes and simmonds for a multitude of purposes were made from straw, heather, floss and practically anything that occurred in long strands that could be wound together. Floss was an extremely useful commodity and one of the old Acts of Shetland stated that no one must cut floss on the scattald before Lammas without due advertising his neighbours under pain of forty shillings (Scotch). In places where there were wide stretches of blown sand the tough stalks of bent were used for making baskets and simmonds and in certain areas it was considered so important that it was shared out fairly among the crofters of the district. In some parts of Dunrossness tussock grass was grown from seeds brought home from the Falkland Islands specifically for the purpose of making simmonds. The introduction of coir in the late nineteenth century gradually replaced simmonds for such purposes as securing thatch and anchoring stacks of corn and hay. But the practice of making simmonds continued much longer, and even now the art is not entirely forgotten.

PEAT WINNING

One of the most abundant of raw materials in Shetland is peat, a thick blanket that covers most of Shetland to an average depth of three or four feet. It is a material typical of cold, damp climates, almost as if nature has sought to make amends for the rigours of these latitudes by an abundance of fuel. Under the cover of heather lies a soft brown substance still showing clearly the remains of the moss, heather and other plants from which it is derived. Deeper down the material becomes compressed and more compact and this layer is easier to cut and also more valuable as fuel.

The Shetland peat cutting implement is the tushkar, consisting of a narrow iron spade with a concave face and a second cutting edge about seven inches long, known as the feather, projecting at right angles. The wooden handle to which the metal cutting part is attached is also concave for a distance of about two feet up from the bottom to help the wet slab of peat adhere to it while it is being lifted out of the moor.

Peat cutting preparations start in March or April each year with the flaying of a strip of turf to expose the moor beneath. Two implements are used in this part of the work—the ripper and an ordinary flat shovel. With repeated strokes of the ripper —a long straight iron bar with a sharp cutting edge fastened at an oblique angle to a wooden handle—a vertical cut is made parallel to the edge of the bank and about two feet in from the face left exposed from the previous season. Then digging with the shovel the strip is divided into rectangular segments still connected on the underside to the living moor. Finally standing down in the gref or pit of the bank the faels are prised up with horizontal cuts of the spade.

The faels are too valuable to waste, and a careful peat digger will replace them in the gref to cover the raw scar left by the previous year's working. Thus as the peat bank progresses across the surface of the moor there is no diminution of grazing area. Unfortunately, until late in the nineteenth century there was little attempt at such conservation, and Dr Hibbert writing in 1816 deplored the careless manner in which the faels were discarded, while the banks themselves were frequently cut across the slope of the ground to trap water and become a danger to animals.

The actual peat cutting starts in May when, or so the old people maintained, the 'oil' rises in the moor. With the right hand held midway down the tushkar, and the palm of the left hand pressing down on the end of the handle, the iron blade is thrust almost vertically into the moor, cutting it into elongated rectangular slabs. Two cuts are made simultaneously by the blade and the feather, and since the other two vertical faces have already been formed during the removal of previous peats the slab is connected only at its foot to the parent moor. A quick outward wrench of the tushkar aiming the effort at the bottom severs the peat, and the complete slab is then lifted and laid flat on the heather on the worker's left hand side to dry.

Once all the top level, or first peat, has been cut and placed in regular rows from the edge of the bank to as far inwards as the arms can reach the caster then tackles the second peat. He is now standing two or three feet below the top edge of the bank on his left, and as the second peat is cut the slabs are built into a wall or daek near the edge of the bank and spaced in such a way that apertures are formed through which the air can pass and aid the process of drying. The top of the daek is bound with slabs of peat laid obliquely along the top which serve as an embellishment besides strengthening the structure. And all this is done by one man with the tushkar alone and without a single peat being touched by hand. It is a job that requires a great deal of practice to perfect.

In deep moors a third layer of peat is found. This is soft to cut, slippery to stand on and sometimes it is best to let the surface dry for a week or so before tackling it. In this case the caster is standing about four feet or so below the top of the bank and the peats when cut are built into a second wall, this time on his right hand side in the gref of the bank, on top of the faels laid down during flaying.

After a week or a fortnight, depending on the weather, the peats are ready for raising and they are now touched by hand for the first time. They are set in little pyramids of three or four peats resting on a central peat lying on its side, and sometimes partially protected by a peat lying on top of the others to act as an umbrella.

The weather during May and June is crucial to the success of the peats. In wet summers they take a long time to cure, but these months usually have a low rainfall, and as the wind blows over the peat bank and through the spaces in the dyke itself the surfaces exposed to the air become dry. The worst that can happen is a period of frost which causes the still damp peats to crumble, especially the all important second and third peats that do not have the fibrous content to bind them.

As the peats dry they have to be turned to expose their wet undersides to the air. During the turning process two raisings are turned into one and after a few weeks the peats are tended again, when several turnings are combined into one roog or pile. Some peats are fit for burning at this stage, especially the third peat, which usually breaks into hard, bluish-black clods. These are carefully placed in the centre of the roogs and protected on the outside by larger peats placed damp side outermost. Finally when the outer skins of the roogs are dry they are all ready to be brought home.

Before roads became common various methods were used in bringing home the peats. Where the peat hill was near the croft the peats might be stacked beside the bank and protected by poans and faels. In this case a tramp to the hill for a kishie of peats was part of the family's daily routine. Even in Lerwick and Scalloway housewives had to combine this with their other duties, and visitors to those places were intrigued by the steady stream of women that trudged up the steep footpaths to the peat hill, returning home bent under the burden of a loaded kishie and knitting as they walked.

Where a stretch of water, either a voe or a loch, lay between the house and the peat bank boats were frequently used to ferry home the year's supply. This mode of transport was inevitable in the case of islands where peat does not occur and where the inhabitants were forced to seek a source of fuel in a neighbouring island. The people of Papa Stour long enjoyed the right to cut peat in the Ness of Aithsness in the parish of Aithsting, while the people of Skerries had an area reserved for their use in the island of Whalsay. The people of Burra Isle had to transfer their peats across Clift Sound from peat banks in the Clift Hills, while the islanders of Trondra were allowed to cut peat in the neighbouring isles of Papa and Hildasay.

In all of these cases peat working had an extra air of uncertainty and involved the islanders in a great deal of work and inconvenience. There was an element of danger on account of the weather, and indeed on one occasion a half-decked boat returning to Skerries after a peat-cutting expedition to Whalsay was overtaken by a squall and lost with all hands.

The amount of work involved in boating peats was incredible. The peats were first of all filled into kishies and carried to the shore, where they accumulated in piles near a steep-sided rock or other loading place where a sixern or a haddock boat could float, if only at high water. When a sufficient quantity was ready the kishies were loaded again and emptied into the boat where the skipper or one of the crew stowed them neatly to fill all the compartments except the owsin room, which had to be kept clear. In many cases the people had to load from a beach, wading out with the kishies while the boat was pushed out into the deeper water from time to time as it settled lower with the weight of the cargo.

When full the boat would be headed for home and the great square sail hoisted on the mast. On other occasions, when light winds prevailed, the boat had to be rowed by two men sitting on the taft in the owsin room and struggling to propel the deeply laden craft through the water.

When the home beach or jetty was reached the whole operation had to be carried out in reverse, the kishies filled in the boat and carried ashore up to the croft, where at last the peats could be built into a stack.

In most parts of Shetland, however, ponies were used to carry home the peats in baskets slung on either side of the animal in nets known as meshies. A special wooden saddle had to be used known as a klibber, the two halves being held together by the klibber pin or vernaggel. Even the lairds and ministers had to burn peat. In 1791 it was written that the gentry resident about Baltasound were obliged to employ from ten to twenty horses for the space of six weeks every year to carry home their annual provision of peats.

The practice of 'leading' home the peats declined with the construction of roads throughout the latter half of the nineteenth century, so allowing horse-drawn carts to take their place. The use of ponies survived longest in the island of Fetlar, and it was only in the 1950s that it ceased altogether.

By whatever means they are brought home the peats have to be built into a stout weather-proof stack. After so much handling the hard blue underpeats have invariably crumbled into little hard lumps, especially prized on a cold winter's night for the intense heat they produce, and these are dumped in the heart of the stack as building proceeds. The less valuable upper peats are nevertheless essential for building purposes. With their high fibre content they can withstand handling and they are used for the outer shell that gives the stack its shape. There is great skill in building a stack—it is an important job never entrusted to a novice. The sides have to taper gently upwards, but the slope must not be too acute or else the bottom will 'run'. A well-built peat stack is a work of art, with the outer peats all standing at the same angle whether vertical or steeply inclined, and the four corners gently rounded to lessen wind resistance. And here some of the ugliest and most unshapely peats have a part to play. The wedge-shaped slabs cut from the

old weather worn face of the bank—the skyumpies—are use-
less for most parts of the stack but ideal for rounding a corner.
Finally the top of the stack is protected by slabs of turf placed
in such a way that rainwater is diverted down the outside of
the stack.

A stack of peats represents the culmination of four months'
work, and it is not surprising that some people today jokingly
remark that most of the heat produced by peat is generated in
the working of them. But until quite recently few people could
afford to burn coal alone, and peat was an adequate and an
inexpensive substitute.

MILLING

The Old Shetland water mill was an indispensable part of the
crofting scene, owned either by individuals or by groups of
crofters. In more populous areas they stood in ranks of three
or more exploiting the same stream. It was of a type once common in many parts of the United Kingdom, but surviving
longest in these northern isles. Elsewhere the vertical mill
wheel transmitting motion through a complicated series of
gears to a pair of horizontal millstones had replaced the more
primitive type, but in Shetland the horizontal mill wheel continued in use, imparting its motion through a simple vertical
shaft to the millstones above.

The actual building was extremely simple—a stone-walled
erection built right across a channel or lade along which a
stream could be diverted. Its walls were low, and it was usually
entered through a door at one end, though at Dunrossness many
mills had their doors in the side walls. Below the floor of the
main compartment was the underhoose which housed the tirl
or water wheel. This was a stout cylindrical piece of wood four
feet long standing vertically and fitted with eight or nine small
boards or feathers inclined at an angle of forty-five degrees to
absorb the momentum of the moving water.

Through the centre of the tirl an iron rod known as the
spindle passed upwards through the roof of the underhoose
joining tirl and millstone. At its lower end the spindle rotated
in an iron plate fastened to a wooden beam known as the sole
tree which thus supported the whole weight of the tirl.

The upperhoose was much larger than the underhoose,

since it was built across the roof of the latter and occupied a portion of the ground on either side of the lade. The lower of the two millstones was embedded with clay in the floor of the upperhoose, and the spindle, passing through a hole in its centre, was finally fastened to the centre of the upper millstone. The millstones were made locally from freestone or from a tough variety of schist known in Shetland as mill gröt. A specially suitable variety of mill gröt was found at the West Neaps and Neaps of Graveland in Yell, and this was the main source of supply for the North Isles.

During milling grain was fed to the millstones by means of a wooden box or trough known as the hopper, which was suspended directly above the millstones by ropes fastened to the rafters. It was square in cross-section, wide at the top and tapering downwards to its lower end, which was open, and delivered the grain into a device known as the shü—a kind of chute which fed the grain into the eye of the upper millstone. The rate of supply was regulated by a wooden turning pin fixed to the front of the hopper and connected to the front of the shü by a piece of cord known as the snivvery. The tightening or slackening of this cord by a mere turning of the pin raised or lowered the front of the shü and caused the grain to run out at the desired rate.

The final part of the feeding mechanism was a piece of wood known as the clapper fastened by a length of cord to the shü. It rested partly on the upper side of the millstone, and being shaken by the rapid motion of the millstone and striking against the shü it made the latter vibrate and caused a continuous flow of grain from the hopper. The millstones were not enclosed in any way and the meal spilled out around their edges on to wooden planks set around the millstones for this purpose. It was gathered up off the floor from time to time and placed in a straw büddie.

The fineness of the meal could be altered by means of a device known as the lightenin' tree, an upright beam fastened to the outer end of the sole tree in the underhoose and passing upwards through the floor of the upperhoose, where it terminated in a cross bar of wood known as the swerd (sword). By raising or lowering the lightenin' tree by means of wedges placed between the swerd and the floor of the upperhoose the separation of the millstones could be altered with a corresponding effect in the fineness of the meal.

Milling was an occupation of the winter months when the streams were running at their highest. Where the stream was normally little more than a trickle its flow was augmented by a millpond, or else the level of the loch from which the stream flowed might be raised by means of a dam. The water was allowed to accumulate during the day then utilized at night.

The natural bed of the stream was blocked by a wooden board and its flow was diverted by opening the kluse or sluice to allow the water to flow along the lade towards the mill. The water was given an added momentum by means of a wooden trough inclined at an angle of approximately forty degrees. After passing through the underhoose the water then rejoined the stream, and it might be used to drive several other mills on its way to the sea.

Many long hours were spent in the mills grinding the oats and bere. It was a slow process, since little more than a bushel of meal was ground in the hour; but the operator could leave the mill for short periods provided there was a sufficient supply of grain in the hopper. On cold nights a peat fire burned on the floor and a pot of tea helped to alleviate the boredom, while if more than one person was present stories and songs helped to pass the time. And all the while in the background was heard the constant clack of the clapper and the monotonous steady roar of the millstones.

More than any other feature of crofting life the mill attracted the attention of visitors to Shetland. Inevitably it was a source of amusement to those accustomed to the large meal mills of Scotland. Sir Walter Scott visited Shetland in 1814 as one of the Commissioners of Northern Lighthouses. At that time there were over 500 mills in operation in Shetland and the one that attracted Sir Walter's attention was that of Clickhimin near Lerwick. He described it as 'a hovel about the size of a pig sty'.

In spite of this and other equally unflattering comments the Shetland mill was a triumph of island ingenuity. The only parts that could not be made by the crofters themselves were the iron sile by means of which the spindle was attached to the upper millstone, the ground sile—the plate on which the spindle rotated, and perhaps the millstones themselves, but all of these were readily available and cost very little.

The Shetland type of mill was once common in Scandinavia and in parts of Britain which had been subject to Norse influence. The Scandinavian origin is obvious, and it is possible to trace it even further to Persia, Syria and other parts of Asia. It may well be a relic of the civilization that moved across Europe following the spread of grain growing, and it is interesting to reflect that Shetland was its last stronghold.

WOOLLEN MANUFACTURE

The two branches of Shetland's woollen industry—weaving and hand knitting—have their origins in the distant past, both skills being practised by the Norsemen, as is shown by evidence from Viking settlements in Shetland. During the period of Norse rule most of the wool was woven into a kind of coarse cloth known as wadmel, and it was in this material that the scat or land tax was paid to the king of Norway. The cloth was fulled or thickened by the action of the hands and feet, while in some cases it was spread along the bottom of a narrow passage among the rocks through which the tide ebbed and flowed. According to Dr Jakobsen places where the latter operation was carried out were named Tavacod, and the name survives at several localities today. The manufacture of wadmel declined steadily throughout the Scottish period and ceased altogether in the eighteenth century, but the production of a kind of cloth known as claith continued throughout the nineteenth century.

Rugs and blankets were also produced locally, and bedspreads known as taatit rugs were still being made at the end of the nineteenth century. The Shetland loom could produce only a relatively narrow strip of cloth but two lengths sewn together produced the completed ground. Yarn for the taats was spun specially thick and dyed in different colours, whereby attractive patterns could be worked into the ground.

According to Dr Hibbert the last use to which these rugs were put was as saddle cloths for ponies when ridden by ladies. The rug was laid on the pony's back under a klibber and the lady rode side saddle using the klibber as a handhold. At a later date many of them ended their days when they were spread on the floor as parlour rugs—a use for which they were never intended.

While the weaving of all kinds of cloth declined in importance the manufacture of hand-knitted garments grew in importance, not only for the production of warm underclothes but also as a means of producing garments for sale.

A great deal of work was required to make the raw wool ready for knitting. It had to be carded, oiled, spun and then twined into worsted yarn. Carding was formerly done by kames, and it was long believed that this method produced better results than any other, but it was a slow process and kames were replaced by steel-spiked cairds.

Carding was a time-consuming task, yet when done by eight or ten women gathered in the but end of a croft house, an essential chore was turned into a social occasion. They sat on wooden chairs with the piles of fleeces beside them, picking up handfuls of wool and spreading it out on the spikes of the lower caird, then drawing the upper caird over it two or three times before reversing the position of the cairds and repeating the process. The wool was then lifted from between the spiked faces and placed between the smooth backs of the cairds where with deft movements of the wrists it was formed into a long rower or roller ready for spinning. By the time the evening's work was finished and the merrymaking was about to commence the floor would be covered in piles of rowers, white, grey, moorit and black all separated according to shade.

Spinning and spinning-wheels played an important part in the lives of women, especially during the winter months, when, like carding, spinning was often turned with talk and laughter into an agreeable pastime. The earliest implement was the spindle, its whorls being found in prehistoric settlements in many parts of Shetland. It was simple to make and it continued in use for centuries. Even in the early nineteenth century it was used by women when all the spinning wheels in the household were in use, and Sir Arthur Mitchell found spindle and whorl still in use in Fetlar in 1864.

No one knows when the spinning-wheel was introduced to these islands. There are references in literature of the early nineteenth century to the 'muckle wheel' that rotated on a pivot on the wall, but by the mid-nineteenth century the elongated Shetland spinney had taken over everywhere. A later introduction was the Scottish type of upright wheel usually referred to as the 'cocked-up' wheel and in Shetland simply called the 'Scots wheel'.

In addition to the great variety of natural shades, bright colours could be produced from home-made dyes. According to Dr Hibbert a purple dye produced from the lichen tartareus was formerly an article of commercial importance. It was known locally as korkelit and was produced by scraping the lichen off the rocks after rain, reducing it to powder, steeping it for many days in stale 'household ley' and kneading it into balls roughly one and a half pounds in weight which could then be dried for sale.

Dr Hibbert also noted that the lichen saxitilis, or 'old man's beard', treated in the same way produced a yellowish or reddish brown colour, while the lichen parietinus, known locally as scroita, produced an orange shade, and a blackish or brownish purple could be obtained from the lichen omphaloides.

Many other plants were used as dyes. John R. Tudor writing in 1881 described how a fine yellow dye could be produced from docken roots, while another shade of yellow came from boiling yellowed grass provided that the garment to be dyed was soaked in a solution of alum to fix the colour. Black was produced either from yule girse (meadowsweet) or from peat earth impregnated with bog iron. The only imported dye was indigo, known locally as lit.

As early as the sixteenth century there was a considerable amount of trade with North Germany and the wool was knitted into coarse stockings for export. When the Hanseatic merchants ceased to operate there developed a considerable trade with Dutch herring fishermen, and before their arrival at Lerwick each summer large quantities of stockings, gloves and nightcaps were made ready.

In 1837 Arthur Anderson, trying to popularize Shetland knitwear in England, presented some fine stockings to Queen Victoria, and two years later Edward Standen began marketing Shetland knitwear in London. There developed a keen demand for shawls, fine stockings, gloves and spencers. The island of Unst soon acquired a high reputation for its shawls of gauze-like delicacy—so light that a full-sized article weighed only two ounces. A great deal of work was involved, and since the knitter could work only for short periods at such a delicate piece of work it might take a year or more to complete a single shawl.

Queen Victoria's continuing interest helped to stimulate demand. She was presented with a shawl on her visit to the International Exhibition at Edinburgh in 1886 and thereafter she made regular purchases. By 1897 a Shetland shawl could fetch as much as forty pounds—a large sum in those days.

Until the 1920s the knitting of patterned garments played a very minor part in the industry. Then came a sudden interest in the old traditional patterns still preserved in many places including Fair Isle, and there developed a colossal trade in pullovers, jumpers, cardigans, berets and gloves incorporating those ancient designs. Again the Royal Family helped to stimulate demand when in 1921 the Prince of Wales wore a Fair Isle jersey when he drove off from the first tee at St Andrews as Captain of the Ancient Golf Club of St Andrews.

Interest in Fair Isle patterns continued, and people began to wonder how these designs with apparently Moorish characteristics came to be found in Fair Isle. Then someone remembered that a Spanish galleon, one of the ships of the defeated Spanish Armada, had been wrecked there in 1588, so there grew up the pleasing legend that shipwrecked Spanish seamen, their warlike ambitions thwarted, gave a lesson in peaceful co-existence by sitting down and teaching the women of Fair Isle how to knit the beautiful patterns.

Imaginative names were given to the intricate designs—the Cross of Castile, the Anchor of Columbus, the Moorish Arrow, the Spanish Mermaid, the Star of Grenada, the Basque Lily. It is now recognized that these patterns have a Scandinavian origin, and while there is very little evidence to relate any of them with Spain, it should be pointed out that there is a belief still held in Fair Isle that a girl who was inspired by the cross painted on the bow of the doomed vessel incorporated it into her knitting and it is still produced today and known as 'the ship pattern'.

Knitting came to have a special importance in Shetland that it had in no other part of the United Kingdom, for it enabled the hard-working women of these islands to ensure that every spare moment was spent constructively, making clothing for their families or knitting garments to be sold to bring a little extra money into the home. In fact they were seldom paid in cash, but instead were given the nominal value of their produce in tea, sugar and other commodities. The merchant had the best of both parts of the transaction, since he got the knitwear cheaply and he made a profit on the goods given in exchange— a system of double exploitation that persisted in some places until well into the twentieth century. In some cases where a knitter needing ready money dared to ask for a cash transaction a deduction was made of three pence for every shilling, or 25 per cent.

In spite of poor prices the women continued to knit, as they sat around the fire, as they walked to and from the peat hill, and as they made a journey by sea. The women of Skerries knitted as they travelled to Whalsay or Lerwick and it was said that in foggy weather they could have a good idea of the distance sailed by the length of knitting produced.

Most knitters derived their wool from their own sheep, and country women who had married and settled in Lerwick and Scalloway used to pay a visit to the district from which they had originated for a few days each autumn, ostensibly to visit their friends but also 'tigging for oo'. And in every house they visited they would receive a fleece or part of a fleece so that by the time they returned home they would have a bag full.

The demand for Shetland knitwear became so great that in the 1890s the practice began of sending the wool to the Harrow Wool Mill at Wick to be spun by machine, and later the wool mills at Brora and Inverness produced practically all of the yarn used in Shetland. The names Hunter and Pringle have long been associated with Shetland knitwear, and far more important to island women than their political points of view was the question whether Hunter's or Pringle's yarn was the better.

The practice of carding and spinning declined steadily throughout the opening decades of the twentieth century, but in all other respects the art of knitting flourished until it became an important industry—the third strand, with fishing and crofting, in the islands' economy.

7

The Work of the Sea

Shetland's special relationship with the sea goes back thousands of years to the first settlers who arrived in their frail boats in Neolithic times, being followed by successive waves of colonists who knew how to handle an oar. But of the boats of Neolithic, Bronze Age and Iron Age man no trace remains, and it was the Norsemen who developed the design of the traditional Shetland boat. Even today, more than a thousand years after the arrival of the Vikings, the double-ended clinker built Shetland boat bears an unmistakable resemblance to the Gokstad ship found preserved in a peat bog in Denmark and dating from about A.D. 900.

The oldest known type of fishing boat in Shetland is the yoal —a type that still survives in the parish of Dunrossness and in Fair Isle. A typical Ness yoal is 15 feet of keel with a raked stem and stern that give an overall length of $21\frac{1}{2}$ feet. Her beam amidships is $5\frac{1}{2}$ feet and her inside depth is a mere $1\frac{3}{4}$ feet. The most surprising feature is the lightness of her framing. At first glance she is an unpromising craft for the waters in which she has to operate, but Ness men claim that her lightness is the secret of her success, since the resulting suppleness makes her a resilient sea-kindly vessel, as buoyant as a gull on the water, and ideally suited for the tide-riven waters around Sumburgh Head.

The dimensions of a Fair Isle yoal are more variable, but the shape is basically the same. John R. Tudor gave a detailed description of one in his book written in 1881 and he described the short chopping stroke used by the oarsmen to get through a tide string. The Fair Isle men used their yoals both for fishing and for trading with passing vessels, and a visitor of 1892, referring to the latter practice, called the Fair Isle boat a 'special temptation of Providence'. At one time whenever a new boat was required the whole male population of the island pooled their efforts and a yoal could be constructed within a week.

The yoal of both districts is built with six planks or strakes fastened to each other by copper nails in overlapping or clinker fashion. In a Ness yoal the boards are named from the keel upwards the ga'board, the hassins, the lower and upper sools, the sand straik and the upper wupp. They are connected to each other by three pairs of timbers known as bands.

The bands divide the boat into four rooms or compartments named the fore room, mid room, oswin room and shot. The latter room serves as a kind of fish hold and the owsin room, as the name suggests, is kept clear for owsin or bailing out the water which comes in over the side while sailing. This is done by means of an owskerri or scoop, known in some places as a kap.

The tafts, or seats for the oarsmen, fit on to the bands and rest on strong horizontal supports known as bekks. Underneath the tafts are small boards known as fiskafjaels that effectively partition off the various rooms. Finally the boards that cover the bottom of the boat and make a level floor to each room are known as tilfers.

The yoal is propelled by six oars, each of the three-man crew pulling a pair. The constant friction of the oar is absorbed by a block of hard wood called the routh fixed into the gunwale by two wooden pins known as routh pins. A vertical block of hard wood known as the kabe, set into the routh, acts as a pivot for the oar and also serves as its forward stop. The oar is held in place against the kabe by a hummlieband—a ring of rope or hide which passes round the oar and through a hole in the routh just forward of the kabe.

When the wind is favourable a square sail can be hoisted on a mast stepped in the mid-taft into an iron strap fixed to the keel. The rigging consists of strouds which are secured to the sides of the boat. The sail is run up the mast by means of a rakki —a horn or hardwood ring to which the halyards are fastened. Stone ballast it carried in the mid room placed evenly along either side of the mast.

A larger version of the yoal evolved in the latter half of the eighteenth century as Shetland fishermen began to prosecute the fishing industry at ever greater distances from land. This was the sixern, so called because she was crewed by six men each pulling a single oar. A typical sixern was 18 to 20 feet of keel with an overall length of 26 to 30 feet, a beam of 6 to 7 feet and an inside depth of roughly $2\frac{1}{4}$ feet. There were six compartments in a sixern; called the fore head, fore room, mid room, owsin room, shot and the hurrick or kannie, the latter being occupied by the helmsman. The shot was the largest of the rooms and was used as a fish hold. The sixerns became larger towards the end of the nineteenth century when vessels with a keel length of twenty-two feet were common.

At first the yoal and sixern alike were imported from Norway as boards already shaped and numbered for assembly in Shetland. This practice ceased in the middle of the nineteenth century, by which time island craftsmen were able to construct their own boats from imported timber or from driftwood.

A smaller version of the sixern was the haddock boat that evolved after 1880, and at the lower end of the scale there has always been a great variety of fourerns or four-oared boats used for inshore fishing, for transport and the numerous jobs required by a people who make their living on or beside the sea. They were ideal boats for rowing, and it was in a craft such as this that around 1850 an elderly woman rowed from Dale of Walls to Foula. The Shetland boat has a marked tendency to seek to windward, and since on the occasion referred to there was a fresh steady wind, the lady made good headway by pulling only one oar on the weather side of the boat. As she put it: 'I rowed on the wan side an' Güde rowed on da tidder.'

Each type of boat was designed for hauling ashore after a trip at sea. They were hauled out of the reach of the waves on flat linns or boards placed to prevent the sharp keel from sinking into the sand or shingle. Slabs of oak greased with rotton droo were especially suitable, but best of all and extremely common on most beaches were the rib bones of caaing whales, which were durable and when wetted offered little resistance to the passage of the keel.

In summer the boats were left to stand at the top of the beach supported by long shaped beach stones or triangular frames of wood known as shoards, or again quite commonly by the skulls of caaing whales, which made an ideal substitute. When bad weather threatened the boats were drawn higher up the beach into specially prepared hollows known as noosts, where they could be firmly secured against the wind.

THE FISHERIES

Until the late eighteenth century, for a visitor approaching Shetland his first impression of island life was gained from scores of yoals fishing several miles from land, their crews busy hauling ling, cod and tusk by handline, while at Dunrossness and Fair Isle large quantities of saithe were taken in the tideways.

In these tiny open vessels they explored the fishing grounds around these islands, and they came to know the underwater features about as well as the features ashore. They soon came to know where the best seats or fishing grounds lay, and these seats were given names descriptive of the type of seabed in that area. Da Skorms was a seat with rough uneven sea bottom (from O.N. *skryma*, or scratch); Da Keldi, off Stenness, is believed to have derived its name from the soft sandy bottom found there (for O.N. *Kelda*, or swamp). The seats nearest the shore were generally known as klakks while those offshore were usually referred to as raeds. The raeds were generally called after their particular meeds or landmarks; e.g. the Hoevdi Grund near Foula is located where the prominent headlands of the North, Mid and South Hoevdi can be seen in line.

Although fish hooks of wrought iron were available in Viking times the people of Shetland could make their own ingenious device known as a snarra pin or bernjoggel. This was a wooden pin with a notch in the middle where the toam was made fast. The bait was tied by a piece of woollen thread known as vaav, which was also used for tying one end of the pin to the toam to enable it to hang in a vertical position whereby it could be swallowed more easily. Whenever weight was applied to the toam, as when swallowed by a fish, the vaav broke, enabling the pin to swing into a horizontal position and stick across the mouth of the fish. By this means the fish could be hauled towards the boat. The snarra pin was widely used in Iron Age times and was still in use in the nineteenth century whenever iron hooks were temporarily unavailable.

As the ling fishery developed in the late eighteenth century the inshore grounds became exhausted, possibly through a climatic change affecting the movements of the fish, and boats had to go farther afield. Larger boats were required, vessels able to sail long distances, to reach fresh fishing grounds and carry sufficient fish to make the longer voyage worthwhile. In this way over several decades the sixern evolved as a larger version of the yoal.

The distant water fishery that then developed was known as the haaf fishing (from O.N. *hav* or open sea) and it was the main industry of these islands throughout most of the nineteenth century. It was prosecuted from stations as near the fishing grounds as possible, the essential requirement being a beach covered in large round stones where the salted fish could be spread out to dry and where the sixerns could be hauled ashore during bad weather.

There were haaf stations all round Shetland, with a heavy concentration at Northmavine, where there were stations at Stenness, Hamnavoe, Heylor, Uyea and Fedeland. There were several in Unst, Yell and Fetlar and the Whalsay men had their stations at Symbister and on the tiny offshore islet known as Grif Skerry.

Preparations for the season began at the end of April when the sixerns were tarred, launched and re-rigged. Then the men had to spend a few days at the station repairing the lodges or huts where they slept and ate their meals when ashore. The fish curers, too, were busy reopening and repairing their premises, ferrying in salt and provisions and scrubbing out the wooden vats in which the fish would be steeped in pickle.

The twelfth of May was the traditional date for the start of the fishing and when in full swing the boats made two trips each week, from Monday to Wednesday and Thursday to Saturday. They rowed or sailed until the highest land in Shetland lay like an upturned bowl on the horizon. While at sea sleeping was virtually impossible and cooking extremely difficult, although each vessel carried a fire kettle and a supply of peats for brewing up a pot of tea. Sometimes the crew members would in turns try to snatch a few hours' sleep rolled up in the sail in the forehead.

There was a place for everything in the sixern. The forehead was used as a kind of store for the buoys and buoy ropes, hand-line reels, the bread box and the blaand keg. As in the case of the yoal the ballast was stowed in the mid room on either side of the mast and the owsin room was kept clear for bailing.

As a prelude to the fishing trip bait had to be procured, and for this purpose many sixerns carried a few drift nets to catch herring. If herring was unobtainable they used whatever was available such as mackerel, conger eels and even yoags. Old men and young boys were frequently employed catching what-ever they could along the shore. Some sixerns carried four had-dock lines which were baited with mussels or limpets carried in a special bait box known as a koopi. When a sufficient quantity of bait had been secured the sixern set her course for the far haaf, which was generally reached late on Monday.

The sail was then lowered and stowed in the forehead and with four men rowing the long fleet of lines or tows was set. Each man's share of the tows was known as a packie and was in turn made up of buchts or hanks of line each fifty fathoms long. The longest fleets of line were those carried by the men who put to sea from Fedeland, where each man's share was 20 buchts or 1,000 fathoms of line. Hooks on four-foot long bids were spaced along the line at intervals of nine yards so that an entire fleet of tows would include 1,200 hooks.

First to go over the side was the buoy followed by a long börop (buoy rope) then the first kappie stane, which anchored one end of the fleet. Then followed the lines, and as shooting proceeded the hooks, previously placed in strict order with their points stuck into a block of cork along one side of the line holder, were lifted in turn, threaded through the half of a herr-ing, haddock or other bait species, and thrown well clear of the boat before the vessel's momentum took up the slack.

When the last hook had been baited, a second kappie stane was fastened to the end of the line with a börop and buoy to mark the near end of the fleet. In case this buoy should disap-pear under the weight of tide a thin line known as a vaarline was made fast between the buoy and the boat. On grounds where the tide ran strong more sinkers known as bighters were used at intervals along the fleet, and at these points extra buoys were placed to assist in recovery should the fleet of lines break.

After this first stage of the operation, which might take three or four hours, the men could have a rest for half an hour or so while the fish were given an opportunity to take the bait. This period was usually occupied in a hurried meal of thick oat cakes known as biddies, or in some places as sea brünnies washed down with blaand.

The meal over, the men prepared for hauling, two of them taking their places at the starboard side of the boat as the sixern was manoeuvred up to the near buoy. One man standing in the owsin room hauled in the line, coiling it as it came into its wooden box. The other man sat astride the taft on the foreside of the shot armed with a knife and cavilling tree which was used to remove the hooks from the fishes' mouths. He also had a huggie staff or clip to lift large fish into the boat and to secure the soond blawn fish—those that had come off the hooks during hauling and which generally floated a short distance from the boat kept afloat by their blown air bladders.

These two men were clad in waterproof garments—long, leather sea boots and joops made of sheepskin which covered their arms and their bodies from the chin to below the knees. In the late nineteenth century home-made garments of this type were replaced by lighter garments made waterproof with boiled oil.

During hauling the other four men rowed the boat back along the direction in which the lines were laid to make the job of pulling in the lines as light as possible. Between 100 and 200 ling was considered a fair haul, but it was often exceeded. Whenever it seemed that they were going to catch more fish than the boat could carry they would let the sixern swing and proceed to gut and head the fish already caught, to reduce the weight. Otherwise they waited until the lines were hauled before starting to clean and sort the catch.

Ling, cod, tusk and saithe were the species most in demand; all other species, being considered of lesser value from an economic point of view, were reserved for the use of the fishermen and their families. Halibut were taken in large quantities but they were unmarketable until the 1880s when improved communications with Aberdeen created a demand for this species. Prior to this time halibut, too, were regarded as a perquisite of the fishermen and at times they were so plentiful that they were used as linns for hauling the boats ashore.

The men had no sleep on Monday night and they were seldom back at the lodges even for Tuesday night. If the weather remained fair the lines were baited and shot for a second time, then at last, with perhaps a ton or thirty hundred-weight of fish on board, the course was set for home. In the early days of the haaf fishing the men rowed whenever the wind was dead against them—they had not learned fully the art of tacking—and the minister of Northmavine, writing in the *Old Statistical Account*, tells of the boats rowing home against a south-easterly gale and the men glad to rest their oars in the lee of the Muckle Ossa.

Back at the beach the fish were first weighed. Ten to the weigh, or hundred-weight, were considered good fish, but sometimes they averaged eight to the weigh or fourteen pounds each —really big fish. Then they were taken and split open from the belly along the backbone (which was removed for two-thirds of its length) and left in wooden vats with pickle for a day or two before being taken and spread out on the clean white beach stones to dry.

The beaches were a hive of activity throughout June and July with a steady coming and going of sixerns, while the fish had to be turned when partially dry and placed under cover whenever it threatened to rain. Dr Hibbert on his trip to Shetland in 1816 visited Fedeland, and he describes in detail the busy scene there as the fishermen and the beach boys went about their work.

Wednesday was regarded as the mid-week break for the fishermen—a chance to eat and sleep in the relative comfort of the lodge. While the rest of the crew tended to the fishing gear one of their members acted as cook. He lit the fire in the lodge, filled the ringlodie or iron kettle with water and prepared a meal of fish and potatoes. The men's wives or daughters frequently visited the station on Wednesdays bringing with them kits full of fresh milk and scones and bannocks to replenish their bread box. In return the women returned home with a variety of unsaleable fish such as halibut and steenbiter (cat-fish) and inevitably a few cods' heads, which were considered a delicacy.

Towards evening the men would stretch out on the long wooden bed that occupied the inner end of the lodge from gable to gable, and enjoy their first night's sleep since the previous weekend. Even then it was not a full night's sleep, since they had to be at sea again early on Thursday morning on the start of another trip which would last until Saturday, when the men could leave their boats at the station and return home for the weekend.

The summer season was interrupted by the Johnsmas foy—a festival celebrated on 24th June. The fish merchant who owned the boats and lines presented each of his crews with a bottle of whisky as his contribution to the festival. The fisher-men's sons were frequently invited to attend the supper which was the main part of the celebration. The lodge kettle—a round-bottomed pot with a capacity of five or six gallons which served such functions as leeping limpets and boiling the meals was well washed out and had milk poured into it. Then into the milk was poured oatmeal to make millgruel. When ready the kettle was set between the earthen binks that served as seats and men and boys sat around the pot and supped from it together.

The Johnsmas foy was a time for looking back with grati-tude on what had gone before and invoking God's help for the remaining weeks of the season. It seems that at the peak of the haaf fishing in the early nineteenth century the toasts were extremely formal and taken very seriously. One recorded by Dr Hibbert runs as follows:

'Men and brethren lat wis raise a helt. Here's first to da glory o' Güde and the guid o' wir ain puir sauls, wir wordy land maister and wir lovin meat midder. Helt ta man, death to da fish, an guid growth ida grund.'

Even at the peak of the fishing season they could not forget the croft.

The haaf fishing ended on 12th August and the occasion was

marked by another foy. Again the toasts reflected the progress
of the crofts, and a favourite toast was:

'Güde open the mooth o' the grey fish (sillocks) an' haud His
haund aboot da coarn.'

The final part of the season was the settling, when the merchant completed his calculations, offsetting the value of the fish
landed against what the men had drawn from his shop and
deciding how much, if any, profit they had made from their
summer of toil.

From the haaf days have come tales of daring and heroism
that would fill several volumes—stories of men exploring the
fishing grounds thirty and forty miles from land in tiny open
boats under thirty feet long. Every district has its stories of the
fleet of sixerns caught by a summer storm, of lines being cut,
the sail being reefed and a homeward path being followed
through a waste of breaking sea.

When running before a gale there were two men upon
whose skill the safety of the boat depended. These were the
skipper, who controlled the helm and the sheet, and the towman, who controlled the halyards of the sail. If a wave should
rise up astern the towman would wait until it lifted the boat's
stern, then he would lower the sail slightly to ease the boat's
motion, then as the wave passed on ahead he would raise the
sail again and the craft would speed ahead onto the harmless
surf of the spent wave. The haaf men knew the importance of
pouring oil on the sea, and at times fish livers were crushed in
the owsin room and thrown on to the troubled waters, the oily
lioom quickly smothering the worst of the breakers.

With wind on the beam the helmsman had full control of the
boat, and could pick his way, estimating where each lump of
sea would break and altering course slightly to avoid it. But
sometimes a lump of water could not be avoided. In these cases
the helm was quickly put up and the boat was set racing away
from the wave, letting it break harmlessly astern. The faster a
boat could run away from a lump the less force would the
wave exert when it caught up with her.

An indication of the incredible amount of experience gained
by the haaf men is the way they could find the shore in misty

weather. They looked for the moder dy—an underswell in the sea that always set towards the land, irrespective of wind or tide. This particular skill was lost when the compass was introduced.

At times not even the skill of the haaf men could bring them to safety and the history of the haaf era is punctuated by disasters. In 1774 George Low stated:

> 'In Northmavine much loss of men at sea. Seldom a year passes but some perish here. A few weeks ago 3 boats with 16 men were lost leaving 11 widows and 46 children.'

The worst disaster of all occurred on 16th July 1832, when thirty-one boats were lost, and although the crews of fourteen were rescued by Dutch fishermen in their large herring busses, 105 men were lost. Again on 4th July 1881, ten boats and fifty-eight men were lost in a sudden summer storm.

The 1881 disaster confirmed what most people had known for years—the sixern was inadequate for the waters in which she had to fish, and her greatest drawback lay in the fact that she was entirely open to every sea that broke over the gunwale. The decline in the haaf fishing began early in the second half of the nineteenth century and it gathered momentum with the arrival of larger fully-decked vessels purchased secondhand from the East Coast of Scotland. For in the 1870s Scottish fishermen demonstrated to the Shetlanders that it was possible to prosecute the herring drift net fishery and long lining for ling and cod from the same boat. So Shetland's fishing industry developed an entirely different appearance, with a new spring fishery for ling and cod and a summer herring fishery that lasted from May to September.

As the decked boats increased in numbers, the fleet of sixerns declined. It was estimated that in the mid-nineteenth century 170 sixerns fished from Northmavine, but by 1887 this figure had been reduced to only thirty. Elsewhere the reduction was as rapid, and in 1894 it was reported that the last sixern at Whalsay had been hauled ashore to make a henhouse.

THE FAROE FISHING

A second branch to the ling and cod fisheries developed in

the early nineteenth century with the introduction of fairly large cod smacks which operated as far afield as Rockall and Iceland, with occasional trips being made to the Davis Straits. But the most common fishing grounds were the banks around the Faroe Islands, hence the name, Faroe fishing, by which this fishing was normally known.

The smacks were owned by curers in Lerwick, Scalloway, Reawick, Voe, Baltasound and other places, and the crews joined them in February to prepare their vessels for the coming season. In March, if the weather was suitable, they set sail for Faroe deeply laden with salt for curing the catch. Provisioning was a lengthy process since they had to carry sufficient food to keep twelve or more hard-working men for a period of up to two months. Bait was usually mussels in bags or barrels, kept alive with frequent dousings of salt water, and the smacks also carried drift nets for catching herring.

When the banks were reached the headsails were lowered, the drogue was streamed from the bow and every man from the master to the youngest deck hand began to bait his line. The gear was a simple form of handline, the fish being caught on a device known as a spread—a heavy lead sinker with a hole through which a length of wire was passed. From either end of the wire was suspended a thick toam with a hook.

While the cod were taking there was no thought of rest. As soon as each pair of cod were removed, the hooks were re-baited, and while the lead was running towards the bottom the captor took hold of each fish and with a knife cut off the beard-like appendage on the lower side of the jaw. This was carefully deposited in a can or other container, where it could be kept as proof of his catch. When settlements were made the men were paid purely by results, and the more barbels the greater was the pay.

Work continued until the smack had drifted off the shoal or until the skipper decided that the weight of fish on deck was making the vessel top heavy. Then the lines were stowed away, the splitting board was set up across the deck and the tubs and draining vats were set up in their appropriate places. The fish were gutted and beheaded by the younger crew members before being passed to the splitting experts who cut the cod open and removed the backbone as far down as the anus. Then after a thorough washing and scrubbing until every trace of blood had been removed, the drained vats of fish were passed into the hold where the cod were packed carefully in layers of salt.

When the last cod had been salted there was time for a proper meal and a few hours' rest before the process was repeated all over again. And so it went on, fishing being followed by salting down, but interrupted by days or weeks of bad weather, until the hold was full or until the provisions became exhausted. Then the smack sailed for home and curing was completed on the drying beaches of Shetland.

After a week's rest while unloading was being carried out the crew made their vessel ready for the second trip to Faroe. It was on this trip that tobacco and brandy were loaded at Thorshavn and the return trip had a more than usual excitement about it as they tried to avoid the revenue cutter.

Many stories are told of how a vessel was caught red-handed and the crew fined or sentenced for their audacity. Many more tales are told of how the Customs officers were outwitted and the kegs of brandy safely secreted in peat stacks and skroos of corn. Some of the smacks could actually outsail the revenue cutter, and in one case the owners were compelled to cut a few feet off their vessel's mast.

The third trip of the season was made to Iceland, and this was often the most successful voyage of all. Landings of 20,000 cod were by no means uncommon, but it must be pointed out that the Iceland cod were usually smaller than those caught at Faroe and Rockall.

In November the smacks sailed to Stromness in Orkney or to some mainland port for their annual overhaul, being slipped to have their bottoms cleaned and re-coated. Then they were either laid up for the winter or spent the next few months as freighters carrying their owners' produce to markets in Spain.

From its peak in the 1860s when about seventy smacks sailed from Shetland the industry declined towards the end of the century. As in the case of the haaf fishing, the rising importance of the herring industry diverted the attention of fishermen and merchants alike, and large quantities of cod taken from the banks of Newfoundland depressed the European markets. There was a revival in the mid 1880s, and in 1896 twenty-four smacks sailed for the cod banks, but by 1899 the fleet had dwindled to seven.

Many of the old smacks, their fishing days at an end, survived a little longer as cargo vessels running in supplies of coal and building materials and Spanish salt used in curing herring. They were small enough considering the waters in which they had to trade, and many were wrecked or lost with all hands. One of the best known vessels, the *Bohemian Girl*, was wrecked near Whalsay, and it is known that her crew survived the stranding but they were all drowned before they could gain the shore.

HADDOCK FISHING

Until late in the nineteenth century the haddock was a much despised species in Shetland. It was caught on small lines for bait and when the weather was fair in winter a few buchts of line shot on the haddock sands could usually be depended on for an abundance of fresh fish. Although the demand for fresh haddock was keen throughout mainland Britain, and English and Scottish inshore fishermen carried on a successful winter fishery, Shetland fishermen were debarred from participation because there was no way of getting the catch to market. At that time communications with the south were limited to one sailing per week throughout the winter, and haddock, even when packed in ice, could only be expected to arrive at Aberdeen or Leith in a fresh condition if caught a day or two before the steamer's sailing day. In 1881, however, a change occurred with the introduction of a second sailing each week and suddenly a steady market was opened for Shetland's line-caught haddock.

The fishery quickly assumed major proportions. A special boat developed—a smaller version of the sixern—known simply as a haddock boat, manned by a crew of four and propelled by four oars or a dipping lug sail. They were generally thirteen feet of keel and many were built at the yards of L. Goodlad, Lerwick, Walter Duncan at Hamnavoe and of Messrs Hay and Co. at Scalloway and Lerwick.

It was a hard life for the fishermen, operating in small open boats in the heart of winter. They shot their lines in the early morning when with the first trace of dawn they were able to identify their landmarks. Then after a short rest while the lines were being 'tided' they began to haul. Catches of five to ten hundred-weight were common and for many years the usual price was six shillings a hundred-weight. Ashore the fish were purchased by merchants who gutted and washed them and packed them in boxes with ice for shipment south.

In this fishery the greatest amount of work was done at home. Since the haddock hooks were too small, too numerous and too closely spaced along the line it was impossible to bait them as shooting proceeded. Baiting was carried out in front of the fire, in the already overcrowded but end. When the fishermen arrived home cold, hungry and desperate for a few hours' sleep their wives assumed responsibility for the lines. Their normal housework had to be performed as quickly as possible, since the wet and sometimes tangled lines had to be redded, cleared of stones and old bait, repaired if necessary and rebaited.

On the west side of Shetland a haddock line consisted of six buchts each sixty fathoms long, and each of the four-man crew contributed three lines to the boat's fleet. Each bucht of line carried approximately 100 hooks, so each household had to bait 1800 hooks each day—double that figure when two crew members came from the same household. A burden fell on the children too, and each child usually had a line to bait when he returned home from school.

The usual bait was the soft flesh of mussels dragged up from the seabed in specially constructed, iron-toothed dredges, Some men actually made their living from dredging mussels for sale to the full-time fishermen. When baited, the hooks were laid in strict order in rows at the mouth of the line skoll, each row being separated from those above and below by strips of wet newspaper which prevented the line from becoming hopelessly tangled during shooting.

As in the case of the haaf fishing and the sixern, it was only the skill of the inshore fishermen and their expertise in handling a boat that made the small haddock boat so effective, but at times not even the skill and determination of their crews was enough, and loss of life was common. All the toil, privation and hardship of the haddock line fishery is epitomized in the story of Laurence Moar of Whalsay. One afternoon in December 1887, he and his crew were hauling their lines as were scores of crews all round Shetland, when they were overtaken by a blizzard and winds of hurricane force. From their position Moar knew that it would be suicide to seek safety at Whalsay and that the only chance of survival lay in running before the onslaught. With the helm held firmly under his arm, with one hand clutching the sheet and the other bailing continuously Laurence Moar brought his boat to Lerwick. Two of the crew were dead from exposure and the fourth man was lying unconscious in the bottom of the boat.

Only when the storm abated and the last battered haddock boat reached its noost was it possible to count the cost. In all twelve men perished that day, including a crew of four men from Spiggie, lost when their boat missed the narrow entrance of the bay and went crashing to its destruction below the grim cliffs north of Fitful Head.

Compared to the haaf fishing the winter haddock fishery has received very little publicity and has not attracted the attention of researchers, yet it too covered an important chapter in the history of these islands, and its main importance lies in the fact that this was the start of Shetland's fresh fish trade, as opposed to the salt fish industry. It was to bring unprecedented prosperity, although not until the open haddock boats had been replaced by large fully-decked vessels powered by petrol-paraffin engines, and lines had given way to seine nets.

SUBSISTENCE FISHING

Fishing operations were not confined to the regular fishing seasons. Throughout the year whenever a chance presented itself the men were out in their small four-oared boats fishing with handlines to keep the house supplied with fresh fish. In many ways the produce of the sea was more dependable than the harvest of the land, and had it not been for the shoals of fish that swarmed around the shores the islands could never have supported a population of 30,000 as they did throughout much of the nineteenth century.

They used whatever the lines or drift nets brought to the surface. In winter and early spring haddock were abundant and gradually improved in condition until spawning time in March. In summer the boats could go farther afield and there was a greater variety including ling, cod and tusk, mackerel and herring. In some years the herring came close inshore in vast shoals and they could be caught by drift net and scoop net, and at times could be taken in baskets from the beach.

It is recorded that the winter and spring of 1868 were very harsh, and nowhere more so than in the island of Papa Stour. On the last Saturday of June, a geo on the north side of the island known as Creed was reported to be full of herring. Holes scooped out of the shingle at the edge of the beach quickly filled with herring and several baskets were taken in this way. Some men came in boats and part of a herring net was set across the mouth of the geo, and when it was hauled it was found to contain the fantastic catch of twenty crans, or something like 20,000 herring. The herring net was of course torn to ribbons, but the island had sufficient food to last until hairst. It is not surprising that the people gathered in church the following day to give thanks to God for their miraculous deliverance from a state approaching famine.

The most reliable source of food was the shoals of young saithe that swarm in the voes in late summer and are found in lesser concentrations throughout the year. They were caught by rod and line from rowing boats, and on fine summer evenings every available boat would be afloat. Two people normally made up the crew, one rowing slowly, keeping the best position near a skerry or underwater rock—a process known as andooin. The person fishing was seated on the after taft with two or three rods projecting over the stern with their inner ends being tucked under the seat. The most common bait was boiled limpets chewed into small pieces in the mouth, by which means a supply of bait was instantly available. Sometimes a white fly was found to produce better results than any bait. A goose pen or gull's feather provided excellent busk for the sillock hooks, but best of all was the white bristles taken from the dorsal fin of a dogfish, left lying a few weeks under a stone near the low water mark, so that all the fleshy part rotted away.

The two grades of fish caught were known as sillocks and piltocks, that is those a year old and those two years old. When taken from a boat the fishing was known as the eela. But this was not the only mode of capture since, unlike other species, they come right up to the rocks, and wherever deep water is found along a steep rock face they can be caught from the shore. Such places are known as craig seats, but the original name was bergset or berset and the form is found incorporated in place names throughout Shetland. Beside many of the craig seats curious cup-shaped hollows are found cut into the surface of a flat rock. They were carved laboriously out of the solid rock hundreds of years ago for the purpose of pounding soe or groundbait—a practice that continued until late in the nineteenth century. Various materials could be used as soe—limpets, crabs and even rooder if nothing else was available. The fish were taken by piltock waands using boiled limpets as bait.

Another form of rock fishing was pocking sillocks, using a pock or dip net. This was a bag of netting attached to an iron ring five or six feet in diameter, suspended by three or more ropes from the end of a wooden pole. The net was allowed to sink and bait was thrown on top of it to attract the fish. At the appropriate moment the pole was jerked upwards to bring the iron ring above the surface of the water. Many tons of sillocks were taken by this method in a typical year, their livers being used to produce oil for lamps.

Even when fishing from the rocks was impossible, as when winter gales lashed the shores, a supply of food was always obtainable from the beaches in the form of winkles, cockles, smirsleens, spoots and other shellfish. Winkles were actually more important as a source of ready cash, being sold to merchants who shipped them out in sacks to southern markets.

Just as nothing was wasted on the croft, so practically every creature of the sea could serve some function in the daily lives of the people. Seals were important for their skins, which were made into rivlins, while in times of extreme famine seal meat was used as food. More valuable still were the caaing whales which appeared in large numbers around Shetland until the very end of the nineteenth century.

Whenever a school of whales was spotted in the mouth of a voe the entire population of every township in the area was thrown into a ferment of excitement. Every available boat was pressed into service—its age was immaterial provided it could float. Then, taking a plentiful supply of stones as ammunition the men set off in pursuit. It was essential to get to seaward of the school without the whales becoming suspicious, then

steadily and relentlessly the school was guided up the voe towards a gently sloping beach where the final stage of the drama
would be enacted.

Occasionally a section of the whales would turn and head for
the open sea, and then began a splashing of oars and a throwing
of stones as the men sought to prevent the majority from following them, while the shouts of the men and the shrill blowing of looder horns added to the confusion. Casualties were not
infrequent, since one swipe of a whale's tail could smash in a
boat's side.

As soon as the whales had been driven ashore, the massacre
began. Each man was armed with a lance or flenching knife or
an old scythe blade kept sharp for such an occasion. Before long
the sea was red with blood as the helpless creatures were killed
and the blubber hacked off in strips. The flesh was not eaten,
and the carcases were left to rot until the scavenging seagulls
had picked them clean.

When all was ready the sale of the blubber commenced
under the control of a clerk who first deducted the cost of
damaged boats and oars as compensation for the owners concerned. Then the laird upon whose property the whales had
been killed demanded a third of the proceeds as compensation
for damage to the foreshore. The remaining two thirds were
divided among the crofters and other helpers according to a
well established scale ranging from the man who had first spotted the school down to the youngest boy participating at the
slaughter. Women were not entitled to any share and the story
is told of how a caa of whales took place when the men of the
township were all at sea. Although the wives were involved in
a great deal of hard work the entire crofters' share went to a
three-months-old boy—the only male present at the kill.

Few beaches in Shetland have not witnessed at some time the
killing of a school of caaing whales. In 1831 over 300 were
driven ashore at Maill's Ayre, Cunningsburgh, and the following year 800 were killed at Channerwick. Some places saw a
caa of whale with surprising regularity. So many whales were
stranded at Sand that the returns to the landlord came to be
reckoned as part of the annual income of the estate. Accord-
ingly when Mr Joseph Leisk purchased the estate a much higher
price than usual was agreed. Unfortunately the whales altered

their habits and for a period of forty years no whales entered the Bay of Sand. This was broken in 1899 when 71 bottle nose whales were landed there, ranging in length from 20 feet and down.

The large share exacted by the lairds was a constant source of friction, and several times the fishermen threatened to refuse the laird his customary share. But the landowners held the trump card, since they had merely to threaten to raise the rent and the men were forced to submit. In 1837 a shoal of whales came into Nesting Bay and some of the whales were shot in deep water to prevent their stranding on the beach. The laird remarked: 'I will pay you for your trouble some other way,' and one man at least had his rent raised by two pounds a year.

It was only when the power of the lairds was broken by the passing of the Crofters Holdings (Scotland) Act in 1886 that the men dared stand up to the lairds and gained for the people of Shetland the right to enjoy the full proceeds of a whale hunt. Unfortunately, the last great caa of whales took place in September 1888 and the few whales killed thereafter brought little financial gain to their captors.

THE HERRING INDUSTRY

Although the Dutch had fished herring around Shetland for centuries the local merchants and fishermen were slow to copy them. There was a sudden rise of interest in the 1830s but the new industry collapsed in 1842 with the bankruptcy of the major firm concerned. During the next thirty-five years the only herring landed at Shetland were caught by sixerns which took aboard a few drift nets for a few weeks at the close of the haaf fishing.

In the late 1870s, however, the industry was transformed with the coming of fully-decked smacks purchased second-hand from the Moray Firth and the East Coast of Scotland. The first boat was purchased in 1877, and by 1885 there were 350 of these vessels in Shetland marking the culmination of a few years of growth that has never been equalled.

At first the herring fishing was divided into two distinct periods. Between May and July the industry was based on the west side of Shetland and off the North Isles from ports such as Scalloway, Burra, Walls, Papa Stour, Hillswick, Cullivoe,

Whalfirth, Baltasound and Uyeasound. Then after a short break in the middle of July when the men changed their nets and got their peats home the boats sailed to Lerwick, which was the main port for the late herring fishery that went on until September.

The herring came to dominate the economic life of the islands. The Shetland fleet was augmented by hundreds of Scottish vessels from every port between Eyemouth and Wick, including those of the Moray Firth and from Ireland and the Isle of Man. In some years over 1,000 boats took part in the early fishing, which until the turn of the century was by far the more important of the two parts.

Everything was done by contract. As early as January each fishcurer would make arrangements for a score or more of boats to land their herring to his firm at a guaranteed price, which seldom exceeded ten shillings a cran. And likewise the shore workers, including the girls who gutted and packed the catch, were contracted to a certain curer. A small down payment of say a pound was made during the winter, and having 'taken arles' a gutter was committed to work for that curer.

The early season lasted only a few weeks, yet the impact on those normally quiet west-side ports was profound, with a constant coming and going of barques and tramp steamers bringing in empty barrels and leaving again low in the water with full barrels for ports in Germany and Russia. It was said that in some seasons there was scarcely a woman left in Sandness during June and July since they were all away gutting herring at Papa Stour.

The most astonishing feature of the herring industry at the end of last century was the sudden growth of Baltasound to become one of the major herring ports in Britain. Within a few years both sides of the voe were lined with wooden jetties and every available space along the shore was occupied with curing yards and fish workers' huts. For six or seven weeks each summer the voe was a forest of masts and congestion became acute as sailing boats sought the jetties of the various curers, and stock boats arrived daily, their decks piled high with gleaming white barrels which would soon be filled with herring and exported to the Continent. In the remarkable season of 1902 Baltasound was not only the chief among the early ports, but it beat its rival, Lerwick, into second place overall. In that year 657 boats were based at Baltasound in the early part of the season and the port's total catch was 114,000 crans.

Between 1880 and the early years of the twentieth century the herring fishing fitted perfectly into the rhythm of the crofting year. A second-hand sailing boat was inexpensive to acquire and cheap to operate. Although a great burden fell on the women-folk at home in running the croft, the men were at home during the crucial times of voar and hairst, and as a special bonus many of them finished their season with thirty or forty pounds to their credit, which was a rate of earning never before experienced in Shetland. Those were indeed the boom years for the crofter-fishermen.

But a change was about to take place, since the steam drifters had made their appearance at Lowestoft and Yarmouth and at ports on the east coast of Scotland, and they soon came to dominate the herring industry at every port in the British Isles. They were expensive to purchase and operate and few crofter-fishermen had sufficient capital to invest in a boat of this type.

The only Shetlanders who had enough faith in the fishing industry and were able to invest in an improved vessel were the men who made fishing an all-the-year-round occupation and they kept alive the tradition of herring fishing in Shetland. Shetland's herring industry did not die, and indeed the most remarkable chapters were still to come, with the rise of Lerwick as the main herring port in Scotland. But for the early ports there was no reprieve, and before long all that was left to remind them of their few years of glory were the rotting timbers of the deserted herring jetties.

8

Superstitions and Folklore

It is clear from the accounts of visitors to these islands, and from the beliefs and customs that long persisted, that to our ancestors the world could not be defined merely in geographical or physical terms. They were obsessed with the unexplained forces of nature and with the much wider supernatural realm which they believed lay beneath and indeed often merged with the material world. Human beings were surrounded by a host of spirits on the land, in the sea and in the air, some of them bearing a recognizable shape but many of them being recognized only through their effect on Man and through opposition to his plans.

The early colonists brought their own supernatural beliefs with them from Norway. There was ample scope for their fertile imagination in the raw, untamed wildness of Shetland, and they peopled the rocks and caves, the lonely lochs and the hills with ogres and sorcerers, trolls and giants, ghosts and grotesque creatures. Some of these beings survived only in place names, but others continued to play an important part in the lives and thoughts of the people until late in the nineteenth century, and even in the first half of the present century they were far from forgotten.

Most numerous were the trolls, known in Shetland as trows —little people who lived in underground caverns in the hills and whose name is perpetuated in places such as Trollhoulland and Trollawater. They were a cheerful, happy people, fond of music, good food and drink and on the whole the relationship between them and mortals could be described as a tolerant and almost peaceful co-existence in which each respected the strength of the other. Nevertheless the people feared them and took care not to offend them by word or deed. When talking about the trows it was usual to refer to them as 'da guid folk' in case any were listening.

The trows disliked the long days of summer, but as the nights lengthened they left their underground dwellings and came down to visit the abodes of men. It was a well-known fact that trows abhorred sloth and untidiness, so everything was set in order before the family retired for the night. Pails of water were carried from the well, the fire was cleaned and rested with fresh peats, the pots and pans were cleaned and set away so that the trows could see that this was a thrifty, well-doing family and when they departed they would leave a blessing on the house. On the other hand, if the house was found in a dirty condition, with the pots and pans unwashed, the hert stane in a state of untidiness, the trows would realize that this was a thriftless family and the house might be 'witched' for a year and a day.

A woman nursing a new-born infant was extremely vulnerable, since the trows might carry off the child and leave in its place a poor, ailing changeling who would remain a cripple or an imbecile until it died. The animals, too, had to be guarded, since the trows might carry off the best cow to provide milk in an underground byre, and they would leave in its place a stock, or almost perfect replica of the real cow which might survive for a few days. Animals found dead in the hills were again mere replicas of the real animals which had been carried off to provide meat for a trowie banquet.

For infants and cattle the precautions took the same form—they were sained or protected by an open Bible, a lighted candle or two oat straws laid in the form of a cross. Trows were powerless when confronted with iron, so in addition a knife or a reaping hook were frequently placed beside the child or animal requiring protection.

Men and women were sometimes spirited away to the abodes of the trows, and when allowed to return home they could usually describe in great detail the splendid furnishings and decorations of the underground mansions. But time passed much more slowly in the realms of the trows, and such people usually claimed that they had been absent for only a few hours when they might have been missed by their friends for up to a year. A woman famed for her expertise as a midwife had just put the supper on to boil when the trows took her away to assist at a confinement. She returned two weeks later, and when she entered the house she asked her husband if the fish were ready for scooming.

Their love of music was well known, and many of Shetland's fiddle tunes were reputed to have been learned outside the trows' homes. Again some trowie tunes were picked up by human beings at their own firesides. On one occasion the laird had asked a well-known fiddler to compose at least five new tunes to entertain him and his friends on Martinmas night. Try as he might, the fiddler was unable to do so, and he became increasingly worried as the deadline approached. Two nights before Martinmas he was sitting despondent beside the fire with his fiddle in his hand when he fell asleep through sheer exhaustion. Then a little man clad in a suit of plaited green straw dropped through the lum and proceeded to dance and whistle a whole series of tunes which had never been heard in the district before.

Sometimes while visiting a house the trows might inadvertently leave behind them a silver spoon or other object, or perhaps a trowie woman taken by surprise while milking in the byre might leave behind her her tiny pail. Articles of this nature never failed to bring good luck to their new owners. Once an elderly couple named Farquhar were fast asleep in their box bed, the doors standing slightly ajar since it was a warm night. The old woman woke up, and hearing a strange crooning sound she peeped between the doors to see a trowie mother sitting beside the fire nursing her baby. The woman's attention was especially attracted by a beautiful little pig or goblet into which the mother dipped her hand to anoint the baby. Quickly coming to her senses, the old woman cried out: 'Güde be aboot me an da pig.'

On hearing God's name uttered the trow and her baby vanished in a flash, leaving behind them the jar of ointment. It was described as a tiny jar of unglazed clay with a capacity of about a gill. People came from far and near to be anointed with the magical substance, yet strangely the jar never became empty. Mrs Jessie M. E. Saxby of Unst claimed that she possessed Farquhar's pig, given to her by one of the old couple's descendants. But she wrote: 'There are quite a number of these pigs in existence purporting to be the original one, so mine is probably as genuine as the rest.'

After the coming of Christianity trows were kept in check by the use of the Scriptures, the open Bible, the sign of the cross and the mention of God's name, but it was only after the Reformation, or so the ministers claimed, that the power of the trows was broken. Nevertheless they long remained a force to be reckoned with, and as late as 1816 Dr Hibbert found that the people still sained themselves whenever they passed a knoll where the trows lived.

In Whalsay it was said that the trows left the island about 1850 when fishermen at sea saw a great commotion ashore 'more like soldiers at drill than anything else'. When they reached the shore there was nothing to be seen, and it was commonly believed that what had been witnessed was the final assembly of the trows before they took their departure. It was said that the trows in Unst were forced to leave that island because they could not stand the preaching of Dr Ingram, the famous Free Kirk minister who died in 1879.

The trows may have been the most numerous of supernatural beings, but by far the most dangerous were wizards and witches—men and women who through being in league with Satan created such difficulties for their honest, respectable, God-fearing neighbours. Cases of witchcraft were numerous in Norse times, and a suspect could clear himself of the charge if he could find five people who would join him in swearing his innocence—a process known as the 'saxter aith'. The Christian zealots of the post-Reformation period were reluctant to let any suspects escape, and in the seventeenth century a large number of so-called witches were burned to death on the hill overlooking Scalloway, but not until the pretence of a trial had been carried out.

The trial of Marion Pardoun, witch of Hillswick, shows the many stages in the detection, conviction and execution of one of these unfortunate beings. It was claimed that while she was going from Brecon to Hillswick the devil appeared to her in the likeness of two corbies which hopped on each side of the way. It was said that all her days she was 'a wicked, devilish, fearful and abominable curser' and that whenever she cursed those to whom she wished ill 'every evil, sickness, harm and death followed thereupon'. She cursed Janet Robinson and 'showers of pains and fits' fell upon her. She merely looked at a cow and she 'crap togidder till no lyfe was leukit for her'. She took away the profit from some bere belonging to Edward Halcro when he was 'dichting it' to steep for malt, and she took away the profit of Andro Erasmusson's kine for no less than thirteen days.

Taking away the profit of the cattle or the crops was a common crime in those days and the complaint could be remedied only by the discovery of the witch. In the case of Marion Pardoun her guilt was readily established, for when milk from some affected cattle was shown to her the owner got back the profit. When another cow produced nothing but blood, the fluid was exposed before her eyes and the animal recovered. In another instance when a cow produced only a fetid liquid, Marion Pardoun was not only made to look at the animal but also to milk her, and a recovery followed.

From all over Shetland stories come of boats being lost at sea through witchcraft. In some cases eyewitness accounts survive of how witches floated a wooden kap or bowl in a churn or tub of water and sat watching as the contents became agitated until finally the vessel whummilled or turned upside down. The kap represented a specific fishing boat out at sea and when it overturned it indicated the success of her evil design. Marion Pardoun used a different strategy to carry out her evil plan. She transformed herself into a pellack whale or porpoise, and coming up under a fishing boat she upset it, whereby four men were drowned. This and other facts emerged at her trial at Scalloway in 1644, and in the face of such 'irrefutable' evidence she was taken to the place of execution overlooking the village and burned at the stake.

The last witches to be burned at Scalloway were Barbara Tulloch and her daughter Ellen King, who were put to death in 1712. But the removal of the death penalty for the crime in no way lessened the prevalence of witchcraft. In 1827 a crofter on the island of Havera found himself in court at Lerwick on a charge of assaulting his neighbour. In his defence he pointed out that it was done under extreme provocation since she had witched him and his cattle. In spite of his plea he was sentenced to fourteen days imprisonment and fined one pound.

In addition to trows and witches there were several other beings once feared but now lingering only in the folklore of these islands. There was Brownie, a domestic trow or fairy whose assistance was deemed necessary in the brewing of ale, in churning the butter and in grinding meal in the quern. In most kitchens a sacrificial stone was reserved for Brownie and when brewing a little wort was placed there, whereas when churning a few drops of milk were sprinkled in each corner of the room. He was also responsible for guarding the corn yard during the winter, and at one time a little stack of bere was set aside for Brownie himself. Brownie had to be humoured and appeased but one had to be careful not to overdo the attention, as indicated in an old couplet:

> When Brownie gets a cloak an' hood
> He does his master nae mair guid!

There was also the njuggle, an amphibious creature which frequented meadows and streams and was never found far from water. He could disguise himself as a horse or pony and appear tame and friendly to entice a weary traveller on to his back. Whenever a careless person did so, however, the njuggle became a different creature. With a roar and a flash of blue flame he would rush for the nearest water, his mane erect and his tail curved up over his back 'like the rim o' a muckle wheel'. Whenever a traveller suspected he was being approached by a njuggle there was a way to set his mind at rest. He should take out his tinder box and strike a light, for it is a well-known fact that the njuggle cannot stand fire.

The njuggle often frequented the millstream, and in the mill itself, in the corner of the looder, there often stood a toyeg—a small straw basket—containing a few handfuls of grain as an annual offering. If this was neglected the njuggle would sometimes creep into the underhoose and stop the mill working by grasping the tirl. He could be dislodged by dropping a firebrand down by the lightenin tree.

A large number of stories related to a race of people known as the Finns who inhabited parts of these islands either before or at the same time as the Norsemen. The name is perpetuated in place names such as Finnigarth and Finnie (Funzie) in Fetlar and Finnister in Nesting. They were accredited with extraordinary powers, and were believed to be able to transform at will into the shape of a fish or a bird and could row to Norway and back between sunset and sunrise, the traditional speed being 'nine miles to the warp [stroke]'.

In most northern counties there are tales of mermen and merwomen and a strange race of seal people. In Shetland all these creatures are frequently equated in folklore with Finns. It was said that the Finns possessed a skin or garment like the covering of a seal. Dressed in these clothes they could take to the water as readily as a seal, but if by chance they lost their skin or had it taken from them they were doomed to spend their time on earth.

A man in Unst found a number of mermen and merwomen dancing on the beach, and beside them lay their sealskins. On noticing him they quickly grabbed their skins and returned to the sea as seals, but one skin lay apart from the rest and the man quickly hid it among the rocks above the beach. Returning to the shore he found a lovely girl walking along the sand anxiously looking for her dress. The story goes on to relate how the man married her and how she became an excellent wife to him. Years later one of their children, playing in an outhouse, found a strange object wrapped in a piece of sacking and hidden away in the loft. She took it to her mother, who recognized it as the dress she had lost. For a time she was torn between her affection for her family and her love for her former husband. The latter proved too strong for her, and putting on her sealskin she plunged into the sea and was never seen again.

One of the best known seal stories is that recorded by Dr Hibbert in 1816. The setting is the lonely Ve Skerries, a group of rocky islets that lie west of Papa Stour. At one time men from the latter island used to visit the Ve Skerries to club seals and skin them for their pelts. On one occasion a group of men had killed a number of seals, but before they had finished the work of skinning them a tremendous swell got up and they had to rush for their boat and push off quickly before it became smashed against the rocks. One of their number was left behind, and since the weather was quickly worsening they were forced to leave him and make for Papa Stour while there was still time.

Towards nightfall, as the man lay sheltering in the lee of a rock, the seals came ashore and set about reviving their insensible companions lying deprived of their skins. Several regained consciousness, but since their skins were missing it was realized they would never again be able to join their companions under the waves. The greatest concern of all was reserved for one young seal who was now separated from his wife since she had escaped when the men landed on the skerry.

Then the seals spotted the unfortunate mortal crouching behind the rock, and one of the old seals went up to him and made a bargain with him. She would take him to his home in Papa Stour if he would promise to restore to her the skin of the young seal so tragically separated from his partner. The man was only too willing to agree, and grasping the neck of the old seal he found himself being carried through the breaking tide lumps on his way home. The seal landed him at Acres Geo, from where he walked over to Hamnavoe and found the skin with the marking which had been described to him lying in a skeo there. He kept his part of the bargain and brought the skin to the old seal, who thanked him and set off once more for the Ve Skerries.

Trows, njuggles, witches and seal people were merely the tip of the supernatural iceberg. They were the creatures that spilled over into the world of men. Underneath was a dark groundmass of shadowy figures sensed rather than identified, and all playing their part in a constant turmoil of opposites— good and evil, God and Satan and Heaven and Hell.

As strange to modern minds as the supernatural creatures themselves were the processes that governed man and his environment and linked the natural and supernatural realms. Many of the diseases that afflicted human beings were believed to have a spiritual cause, and weird and wonderful were the methods of curing them. Toothache, ringworm and painful burns were all 'telled oot' by wise women using charms and incantations handed down for hundreds of years. They could cure sprains by a woollen thread spun from black wool and tied round the affected part. This was known as a wristen treed, and it was in use, no doubt infrequently, at the end of the nineteenth century. Three knots known as aaba knots, each consisting of three hitches, were cast on the thread, and each day one hitch was removed by the practitioner, who blew upon it as she did so. When all the knots were removed the sprain was cured.

The number three, and especially three times three, figured largely in magical cures of this nature. The best tonic for an ailing child rescued from the power of the trows was a concoction known as the nine midders' maet, made from food offered by nine women whose first born children were sons.

Old customs took a long time to die. Right to the end of the nineteenth century witches continued to take the profit from the churn, so that instead of butter, a residue of sour milk and water appeared. They made wells dry up in summer and caused fishermen to have many fruitless trips to sea. They could change their shape and turn into beetles, in which guise they would eat the young green shoots of oats and bere in a neighbour's field and leave bare patches on the rigs. Even today when witches have disappeared, and biological and chemical processes determine the success of a field of grain, the beetles are still to be found, and are often referred to as witchie clocks.

In *Shetland Folk Book* Volume IV there is an eyewitness account of witchcraft at work, or rather the procedure followed in order to restore milk to a cow which had sickened through witchcraft. It is difficult to believe that this took place as late as the mid 1920s.

In spite of the efforts of nineteenth-century ministers it was a long time before the last of the trows were banished from these islands. Trowie stories continued to be told by old people who still believed in those creatures, much to the amusement of their less credulous neighbours. Even in the 1950s there was an old man then living in Scalloway who maintained that the best safeguard against trows was a sheepdog coloured black and tan.

SEA LORE

While many of the old beliefs and customs died out, or at least lessened their hold, during the nineteenth century, the ritual of the sea maintained its hold until comparatively recent times, and even in the second half of the twentieth century a few of the observances are still respected, although in a much modified form. The fishermen were the people who faced the greatest dangers and the greatest uncertainty. They could never be sure that they would return with a payable catch of fish; indeed they could not be sure that they would return at all. Whenever something went wrong they would try and reconstruct the previous course of events to determine what had been the cause of their misfortune, and gradually after a long process of trial and error, there evolved an elaborate set of rites and rituals with a right way and a wrong way of doing everything.

When a new boat was acquired the services of an expert were often called upon to examine the boards in order to take a peep into the future and perhaps prevent a tragedy. He studied the grain of the wood and the round knots formed while the timber was part of a growing tree. The presence of windy knots or watery swirls indicated that the boat was liable to be destroyed by a gale or lost at sea. On the other hand there were lucky knots shaped like a fish, and boats that possessed those marks were sure to have more than their fair share of good luck.

On one occasion an old man, after examining the boat, pronounced his verdict as follows: 'Du mey hae a heavy haand but never a faint hert. Water'll no hurt dy boat but wind will. Tak my wird and shoard her weel.' For nearly ten years the boat fished successfully, and at the end of every trip she was yarfasted in the winter noost. But one night in September after a night at the eela her crew intended to make an early start next morning for the ling raeds. For convenience the boat was shoarded just above high water mark but before morning the old man's words were remembered, when a sudden squall struck the boat, turned her right over and smashed her side in against a sharp pointed rock.

Even when going to the boat carrying their sea clothes and fishing tackle the fishermen were on their guard, since certain people were unlucky to meet—those with the reputation locally of having an ill fit or an evil eye. No one should cross the path of a fisherman and walk between him and the sea, since to do so was a sign that the person wished ill to befall the crew.

Even a mundane task like pushing the boat off from the beach had its own set of rules to be observed. The boat had to be turned sungaets—with the sun—never in the opposite direction which was known as widdergaets. It is suggested that this may have been a relic of a form of sun worship as practised by our ancestors of ancient times.

As they rowed off from the beach everything took on a different aspect. They were almost entering a different world, divorced from the day-to-day experiences of those who spent their lives ashore. Just as the land was dominated by numerous creatures and spirits, so the sea had its own race of spirits, and man, in entering a hostile world, had to take care not to offend the forces that operated there.

Men could never be certain whether the spirits of the sea were well disposed to those of the land, so he had to watch what he said. While it was perfectly in order to talk of things pertaining to the sea, or the weather, the fishing grounds and the prospects for a good catch, reference to animals, people and things ashore had to be made carefully and sparingly, and they should never be called by their land names.

So there grew up a form of language with a rich vocabulary reserved for use at sea. Animals and things were referred to allusively using words that described their peculiar characteristics. The cow was called 'a boorik' or 'da brülik', the horse 'da russi' or 'da gjonger', the dog was called 'da rakki' or 'da benebiter' while the pig was known as 'da hirki'. The cat had a whole range of sea names varying from district to district. It was known as 'da foodin' (light footed animal)', 'da voaler' (wailer), 'da spjaaler' (player) and more commonly as 'da skaavin' which means the shaver, the name being derived from the cat's habit of washing its face with its paws. It is significant that many of these words are derived from the old Norn language brought by the earliest settlers from Norway, and this indicates both the great age of the custom and the conservatism of the fishermen.

At sea the North Isles fishermen referred to fire as 'da birtik' (for O.N. *birta* meaning bright). In the same way the sun became 'da gludder' or 'da faiger' and the moon 'da gloamer'. Even such familiar things as the mast and sail had their own special names while at sea, the former being known as 'da stong' while the latter was 'da skegga' and latterly 'da cloot'. The knife used in cutting bait was known as a 'skuni' and the bait itself became known as 'da neebird', while the phrase 'cut the bait' became 'snee da neebird'.

The church and its offices were never called by their proper names by fishermen. In this there may have been a lingering fear that these were symbols of the new religion to which the sea spirits might not have become reconciled. The church was 'da beni hoose' (prayer house) while the minister was 'da upstander' or 'da predekanter'. At sea a man could not even refer to his wife unless in an allusive way, so she became 'da frö' or 'da haimelt'.

While fishing there were certain points to be observed. Hauling was done in profound silence, but when peering down into the water the man at the line could see a speck of lighter green coming nearer until it resolved into the shape of a fish, he was allowed to say, 'Light idda lum'. Should a second be spotted before the first was on board he could inform the others by saying: 'An white anunder', while a third fish was notified with the phrase, 'An white anunder white' and a fourth was signalled with the word 'wheeda'. While there may have been variations throughout Shetland, this was the convention adhered to in North Yell as recorded by Mr Andrew Williamson.

The main species sought were of course ling, cod, and tusk. Halibut were numerous but they were virtually worthless except as food because they could not be salted and could not be got to market in a fresh condition. Nevertheless the halibut was considered a lucky fish and its blugga bane was often stuck in the wall of the lodge and stuck under the after hinnie spot of the sixern for luck. It was considered unlucky to burn the halibut's bones in accordance with an old couplet:

> Boil me an ate me but burn no me banes
> An' ye sall never want me fae your hert stanes.

In spite of his lucky reputation the halibut too had a different name while at sea. He was 'da baldin', or 'da glyde shield', and in some places he was awarded the supreme honour of being called simply 'da fish'. He was a difficult fish to deal with, since he could rush towards the seabed, forcing the man hauling to let go the line. When this happened the man would shout 'haltagonga'. To use the English words 'stop running' would have been futile, but when spoken in Norn it was believed to prove effective.

Quite apart from mixed fortunes on the fishing grounds and the danger from wind and wave, there was a constant threat from creatures of the deep. Whales were common visitors to this area, ranging from the smaller varieties such as the lesser rorqual to the large sei whale and giant blue whale. There were also less readily identifiable creatures, such as the bregdi which chased boats at sea and when it had overtaken one of them it would wrap its long fins around the boat and drag it under the sea. Fortunately, the bregdi could not stand iron, and when the crew slashed its fins with a knife it usually sank out of sight. There was also a creature known as the kraken or the horven, which was reputed to be as large as a floating island, and a variety of sea snakes were sighted from time to time.

These creatures were not confined to the dim and distant past. Sightings continued to be made by fishermen who went to sea in the stoutly-planked, fully-decked vessels that arrived in Shetland in the 1880s. One day in June 1882, the Lerwick boat *Bertie* was lying fishing twenty-eight miles east-south-east from Fetlar when her crew saw a huge creature approaching them 'like three small hillocks on top of the water', each of them as big as a sixern. They thought at first that the humps might be three finner whales, but when they sank simultaneously they realized the protuberances were part of a single animal.

The creature surfaced again, straight ahead of the boat and bore down on them with its mouth wide open. And what a mouth! It was square 'like a table', the upper lip being about four feet thick, and from the lower jaw hung waving whiskers of a sea-green colour and seven or eight feet long. One man said it could have swallowed the boat, and he was careful to add 'with the mast laid'. The head was covered with great barnacles as large as herring barrels, and the length of the animal appeared to be about three times that of the boat—about 150 feet altogether. The men threw cappie stanes at it which bounced off its scaly back like marbles.

As the monster came towards them one of the crew got hold of a fowling piece and sent a charge of double swan post down its throat. This proved effective, for the monster was not seen again. Nevertheless the crew were so terrified that they cut their lines and made for the shore.

The *Bertie's* serpent was only one of several monsters seen at the end of the nineteenth century. Another serpent appeared to the crew of the Peterhead boat *Morning Star* fishing out of Cullivoe. It was forty feet long and had lumps on its shoulders as large as barrels. And in March 1895 the Buckie boat *Campbells* saw a creature off Noss which they estimated as being as long as half a dozen herring nets. Since each net is twenty fathoms long, its total length would have been 720 feet.

It is impossible to separate fact from fantasy, and it has been suggested that to men who were tired after long sleepless nights at sea, especially to men who were by nature superstitious, ordinary objects would at times appear quite different, and that if one man said he saw something, all would declare that they could see it. Nevertheless there is no doubt that the waters around these islands were in some ways more dangerous than they are now. In August 1896 the Peterhead boat *Monarch* was sunk while riding at her nets east of Lerwick after being struck by some large creature. In July 1891 the sixern *Lizzie* of North Roe went missing with a crew of seven. The weather was fine, and it was suggested that she might simply have taken too many fish on board. Two weeks later she was found floating bottom up in Papil Bay, Yell, and when beached it was found that some of her planks were stove in forward, and embedded in the cracks were pieces of whale skin.

Since the coming of steam propulsion, which was in turn superseded by the internal combustion engine, much of the uncertainty has been removed from fishing. It is now a highly scientific operation and there is little place for superstition. Nevertheless there is still a lingering suspicion that it is unlucky to meet a minister while going to your boat or to have one at sea as a passenger. Practically every boat is equipped with radio-telephone and there is no topic which cannot be discussed when it is required. The old taboos are almost forgotten, and the main reason for this is the great advance in the design and construction of fishing vessels. Men who went to sea in tiny open boats with a foot or less of freeboard could not afford to take chances.

WEATHER LORE

To a people who made their living from the land and from the sea a sound understanding of the weather was all important. They studied it closely, and much of what they learned is pure scientific observation although mingled with myth and strange beliefs. They watched the movements of plants and animals and some people maintained that they could read signs of impending change from the way the curldodies and kokkiluries behaved. It was taken as a sign of bad weather coming when the sheep sought their büls in the hills, and very often they sought places which were not immediately sheltered but which they knew would be so when the wind changed.

Birds were invaluable in indicating a change of weather. It was a good sign to hear cocks crowing after sunset, and most important of all were the sounds and movements of the rain goose, the red-throated diver:

> When da rain güs gengs ta da sea
> Draw up your boats anunder da lea.
> But when da rain güs gengs ta da hill
> Draw doon your boats an geng whaur ye will.

Cocks crowing or hens stirring while it was still raining was a sign that it would soon be dry.

Inside the house itself there were numerous signs for those skilled in interpreting them. Sparks flying in great numbers from a peat fire indicated the start of frosty weather, while spunks adhering to the bottom of the cooking-pot indicated snow in winter and cold windy weather at other times of the year. The cat sitting beside the fire gave a large number of clues, for when it sat with its back to the fire it presaged cold weather, and when it washed its face with both paws it indicated the coming of rain. It was a good sign when the cat slept with its head curled up under its paws—'sleeping on her harns', as the old people used to say. And there was a belief that when a cat washed the top of its head the gales would die down—'When a cat washes abüne her lug dan it's for fresh fish da moarn.'

Each day of the week had its own importance in interpreting the weather. A change for the better on Sunday was a favourable omen, but a too bright Monday was a sign of bad weather for the rest of the week. Wednesday's weather was said to be true, while Friday was a day of extremes—either the best day or the worst day of the week.

There were signs to be interpreted in the sky and in the sun and the moon, most of which were based on hard scientific fact. The people watched for white streaks across the sky known as wadder heads, which indicated the direction from which the new weather pattern was being set. A streak running from north-east to south-west was generally taken as a good sign, while from north-west to south-east was a sign of bad weather coming.

Haloes round the sun or moon, known as brochs, were studied carefully since they often foretold very stormy weather. But if the sun or moon 'shone it out'—that is the halo disappeared before the sun or moon set, there was nothing to fear, hence the rhyme:

> When da sun sets in a broch
> He'll rise in a slauch
> But if da broch dees awa
> Ere he sets ida sea
> He'll rise ida moarnin
> Wi a clear e'e.

The brynig—part of a rainbow seen standing on the horizon —foreboded squally weather, and still another indicator of the kind of weather to be expected was the ga or 'mock sun' which could appear on either side of the sun. If it appeared to the right-hand side it was regarded as a bad omen, but if to the left of the sun it need not be feared.

It was not only the weather that had its signs and omens, its rhymes and wise sayings. Every task, from riving flaas to setting eggs, from digging the ground to sowing the seed, had a right and a wrong time for doing it. There was a rhythm in the daily, weekly and yearly round to which an older generation was perfectly attuned and which is no longer discerned in this more scientific but far less practical age.

9

Shetland's Calendar

Life in Shetland may have been hard but it was far from monotonous. The year was punctuated by an incredible number of
special days, and scarcely a week passed without some festival
being commemorated. The oldest festivals had their origins in
Norse times and there was also a large number of saints' days
that somehow survived the change from Roman Catholicism to
Protestantism. Finally there were dates noted for some purely
local aspect of the year's activities and several rees, or spells
of bad weather associated with certain periods of the year.

To complicate the issue, there were two calendars in use, for
when in 1752 Britain adopted the Gregorian Calendar in place
of the Julian Calendar, and in doing so deleted eleven days, the
people of remote parts of the country refused to conform.
Therefore all the many festivals and special days, although
observed in the 'new' style by people such as teachers, ministers and other recent incomers, were not observed by the mass
of the people until eleven days later. In discussing these dates
it is frequently necessary to differentiate between the new style
(N.S.) and the old style (O.S.) eleven days later.

To add further confusion, some parts of Shetland observed
their festivals twelve days after the corresponding dates in the
new calendar. It is almost certain that this difference of opinion
was introduced in 1800, which would have been a leap year
under the rules of the old Julian system but was not deemed
so under the Gregorian order of things. At any rate the people
of Unst celebrated Christmas on 6th January and New Year's
Day on the 13th, and these remained in force until the old

system finally fell into oblivion quite late in the twentieth century.

THE FESTIVALS OF SPRING

As in many parts of the Continent there was a belief in Shetland that mild weather on Candlemas Day—2nd February (N.S.)—was a bad omen. An old rhyme runs as follows:

> If Candlemas Day be bright an fair
> Half o da winter's tae come an mair.
> But if Candlemas Day be dark an dull
> Half o da winter wis dune at Yule.

On Candlemas morning young girls would go outside the house and follow the first crow they sighted, watching with interest where it alighted, for it was believed that it would settle on the house of the man that they would marry. Candlemas also enabled you to get a prediction of your life expectancy. If the first person you saw was coming towards you, only a short life lay ahead of you, but if that person was going away from you, then you could expect a long life.

Candlemas was the reference point for a whole host of special days leading up to Easter.

> First comes Candlemas an dan da new müne,
> Da first Tiesday efter is Fastern's E'en.

Fastern's E'en was the equivalent of Shrove Tuesday and it was marked by a special supper consisting of brose and the half of a cow's head—an appropriate meal considering the time of privation that would follow. The period from Fastern's E'en to Easter was known as Da Lentern, which in Catholic times was a time of sacrifice and of doing without meat. Even after the end of Roman Catholicism in Shetland it continued to be a time of penance, not from religious conviction but because the previous year's harvest was nearly exhausted and the little that remained had to be set aside as seed.

Bogel Day on 17th March (28th O.S.) was an important date, since although too early for the main sowing it marked an important ceremony with the ritual sowing of grain on a small patch of ground known as the Bogel rig. The progress of the rig was carefully watched during the coming weeks and months, since on the success of this sowing depended the success of the main crop to be sown later. On Bogel night burstane made from bere grown on the Bogel rig the previous year was baked into special bannocks known as bogels and eaten by the family as they sat at supper. In this way they marked the continuity from one growing season to the next. The custom lasted a surprisingly long time, since the late George Nelson remembered people in Tingwall sowing their Bogel rig in the early part of the present century. But they did it secretly, as if they would have been ashamed to be caught doing it.

Another festival of March was Lady Day (often known as Marimas) on the 25th, while the last three days of the month were known as the Borrowing Days, although why they were borrowed or from what is rather obscure. According to one version March borrowed three days from April, to enable the former month to extend its period of boisterous rule. Another version maintains that March borrowed a day each from May, June and July and that the weather conditions on the last three days of March somehow indicate the kind of weather to be expected during those three months. At the end of March a period of extremely stormy weather can be expected, and this used to be known as the Bogel ree.

Holy Week was observed by a whole range of festivals. Six weeks after Fastern's E'en came Skuir Fuirsday, Good Friday, Paes Saturday and Paes Sunday (Easter). On Paes Saturday boys went from house to house collecting hens' eggs in the toe of an old stocking. That night the eggs were hard boiled and sometimes painted in bright colours ready for Easter Sunday, when they were taken to a suitably steep grassy brae to be rolled. This proved to be one of the most durable of all old customs, since as late as the 1940s the children of Scalloway still collected their Paes eggs on the Saturday before Easter. It survived longer in the island of Papa Stour, where the eggs were rolled as part of a family picnic on Easter Sunday, and the custom still continues in the islands of Burra and Whalsay.

The last festival of spring was Simmermill Day on the 14th April, a date much looked for since it marked the start of the summer half year. By this date all the seed should be in the ground to ensure the maximum benefit from the growing season. The weather on this day was carefully watched, since it was believed to indicate the kind of weather that would prevail during summer.

THE FESTIVALS OF SUMMER

Beltane on 1st May (12th O.S.) used to be an extremely important festival with a special feast known as the Beltane foy, when bonfires blazed on the hills and men and boys alike danced around them, displaying their agility by jumping over the flames. The fishermen had their own foy to mark the start of the haaf season, when each of the six man crew brought a wife, a sister or a daughter to a party in the skipper's house. During the meal they drank to a successful catch of ling with the toast: 'Death to da head 'at wears nae hair'. Before dispersing, their thoughts turned to the growing crops as well as the fishing grounds with the toast: 'Güde haud his haund aboot da coarn an blaw da bait idda fishes' mooths.'

Beltane had its ree, or period of stormy weather, as if the spirits of the sea, annoyed by all the re-rigging of boats and repairing of gear, were reminding mere mortals of the dangers they faced. It was a time to proceed with caution, as is shown by the old saying: 'Da Beltane ree will mak wis dree'. A few days after Beltane came the festival of Korsmas, a half yearly feast in the Roman Catholic Church also known as the Invention of the Cross as opposed to the autumn festival of Korsmas on 14th September, which was otherwise known as the Exultation of the Cross.

Bonfires blazed again at Johnsmas on 24th June in honour of the sun who was then at the peak of his power. Or were they intended to counteract the effect of witches, who were said to be especially active at this time? Johnsmas, or the Feast of St John the Baptist, was the great festival of the Dutch fishermen who called each summer at Bressay Sound, for Johnsmas signalled the start of their own North Sea herring season. Many aspects of Johnsmas, including bonfires and children's parties, continued in parts of Shetland until between the wars, and even now the festival is not entirely forgotten.

This was also the time for one of the most delightful of all the old customs, when a lad and his lass would each pick a stalk of ribwort plantain and after removing the tiny florets would lay the heads together under a flat stone. If the florets should reappear before the heads withered it was a sign that the couple would indeed marry. It is difficult to understand how the heads could produce fresh florets unless some of them, not fully formed, had been overlooked by the lovers.

The 4th of July was known as Martin o Bulliamas day—a corruption of St Martin le bouillant (boiling), or in other words the hot season feast of St Martin as opposed to the winter feast of St Martin usually known as Martinmas. Again the weather on this day was carefully studied, since rain on this day presaged forty days of rain.

THE FESTIVALS OF AUTUMN

Lammas on 1st August (12th O.S.) brought the haaf fishing season to a close. The boats were hauled ashore and whummilled in their winter noosts, and before the crew finally dispersed another foy was held in the skipper's house. It was a time of giving thanks to the Almighty who had brought them through all the dangers of the fishing season and they implored His help in ensuring a successful harvest of the land. A favourite toast was: 'May da Lord open da mooth o da grey fish (sillocks) an haud his haund aboot da coarn'.

Unlike the people in other parts of Scotland the Shetlanders could not regard Lammas as the start of harvest. No two years were alike, but it was seldom that the corn could be cut before the end of September. Matjomas Day (St Matthew's Mass) on 21st September was a testing time for the crofters, since it coincided with a period of stormy weather nowadays equated with the equinoctial gales, which could flatten and twist the ripening grain. An old saying referred to this threat:

> Matjomas comes in wi his flail
> An hits da aets apo da tail.

But then on 29th September came Miklslmas or Michaelmas, when, it was believed, the corn had derived all the good it was going to get and should be cut without delay. On this date the sea trout had reached the tops of the burns to spawn, 'as heich as ony ram ida hill'. And talking of rams, a male of the flock was always selected at Miklsmas for slaughtering.

Autumn was brought to a close with the third weekend of October, which was known as Winter Saturday and Winter Sunday. It was regarded as a sign of a severe winter to come if the migrating flocks of snaafool (snow bunting) were seen before Winter Sunday.

FESTIVALS OF WINTER

With the arrival of the long dark nights the people had to devise their own forms of entertainment, and every excuse for merrymaking was eagerly seized. While summer's festivals were observed hurriedly so as to waste as little precious time as possible, those of the winter months were prolonged as far as possibly and savoured until the last ounce of enjoyment could be extracted from them.

First came Hallowmas on 1st November (12th O.S.), at one time one of the most notable festivals in the island calendar. The preceding night of Hallowe'en was a time for peeping into the future for information regarding one's prospects for love, prosperity, life and death. A relatively harmless form of augury was known as drappin glesses—dropping part of the white of an egg into a glass of water, when a person skilled in this art would examine the resulting shape and interpret the signs.

A girl, anxious to discover the identity of her future husband, would go alone to the back of the barn and climb to the top of the kiln to cast da clew, or drop a ball of wool down the opening while holding the end in her hand. As she rewound the ball she would call out: 'Wha hadds my clew end?' She was supposed to hear the voice of her future husband answering her out of the darkness.

There were other forms of divination which few dared risk because of the seriousness of the outcome. One was known as passin da harrow, when a young man would lean a harrow against a corn stack, and removing his clothing he would name the last person to have been buried in the local churchyard and push his head through the bars of the harrow. He expected to have a vision of his future life, and especially the way he would meet his death.

A feature of Hallowmas was the foys and banquets, for

which young lads spent several nights beforehand in preparation. They banded themselves into squads, and wearing strange dresses made from straw they went from house to house as skeklers. One of their number carried a kishie in which he collected the burstane brünnies, the sparls and the tees of reestit mutton that the people donated. On Hallowmas Night they repaired with their girl friends to the largest barn in the neighbourhood and spent the night in dancing, laying up guddiks and playing such games as wads (forfeits).

When Hallowmas was past the winter's duties were resumed, and whenever the weather was suitable boats were launched for handline fishing to ensure a plentiful supply of fish for Yule. The only interruption was Martinmas on 11th November which was observed mainly as a legal term day, although the name is remembered in the word mert which was a fat ox slaughtered about Martinmas for salting as a winter standby.

YULE

In Viking times midwinter was enlightened by the great festival of Jul, a celebration that went on for twenty-four days and marked the winter solstice when the sun began his slow return to the frozen Northland. It was marked by feasting, ale-drinking and general merrymaking. With the coming of Christianity the midwinter festival of Christmas was introduced in its place, but it is not surprising that in northern countries much of the merrymaking of the old heathen festival became attached to the new festival, while in Shetland the festival picked up purely local variations along the way.

It is clear that until the end of the eighteenth century, and perhaps later in some places, Yule was a prolonged celebration lasting the full twenty-four nights as in the days of the Vikings, and on each of those nights, Sundays excepted, a rant was held in some house in the community. We are indebted to Mrs Jessie M. E. Saxby of Unst, who wrote down her recollections of Yule as she remembered it in the mid-nineteenth century and as it was described by an older generation.

The first observance was Tul-ya's E'en, seven nights before Yule, and on that night it was believed that the trows received permission to leave their underground abodes and visit the homes of men. One of the most important of all Yuletide observances was the saining required to guard life and property. Tul-ya's E'en was followed by Helya's Night, when a special meal of milk brose was eaten and the children were committed to the care of Midder Mary (the Virgin Mary)— another relic of Roman Catholic days which survived a surprisingly long time. Next came Tammasmas E'en which was particularly holy and no work of any kind was permitted that night.

According to Mrs Saxby, the Sunday before Yule was called Byana's Sunday, and that evening half of a cow's head was boiled and eaten for supper. The skull was carefully cleaned and with a candle stuck in the eye socket was laid aside to be used a few days later.

Yule E'en was a great time of preparation for the main festival of all. After the ordinary bread was baked, a round oatcake was kneaded for each child, varying in size according to age. The cakes were pinched into points around the outer edge and a hole was made in the centre. Those were called Yule cakes, and were no doubt originally symbolic of the sun now returning to the north.

On Yule morning the head of the house rose early and lit the candle in the eye-socket of the cow's skull. Next he proceeded to the byre and fed his cattle, giving them a little better food than usual. Then he went round the house with a bottle of spirits giving each person a dram with the words:

> Yule gude and Yule gear
> Follow de trow da year.

Breakfast was eaten by candle light, and on this occasion bits of candle that had been carefully hoarded for months were produced to make a real show. No work was done on Yule Day but a game of football kept the men busy for most of the daylight hours while dancing was the amusement of the evening.

It is not certain whether all of these customs were observed throughout Shetland or whether some were limited to the North Isles. It is known that some parts of the Mainland had different customs, while the smaller isles had their own ways of celebrating Yule. In all parts of Shetland the day was marked by an abundance of food, while the peat fire blazed almost as

high as the crook bauk. Drink in the form of spirits was scarce
throughout the year but every family managed to procure a
bottle for Yule.

An important feature of Yule was the ball game played on
a level piece of ground usually known as the links or the ba'
green, and which continued for several hours. The ball was a
pig's bladder in a leather cover made from four quarters of
leather—seldom the shop bought variety, but usually the home-
tanned leather produced from the hide of a cow or pony. In
some parts of Shetland the game may have been little more
than a disorganized kicking of the ball, but in many places it
was a proper game with definite rules and known as the game
of doors.

In some parts of Shetland a fiddler went the rounds of the
houses wakening each family with the strains of 'Da Day
Dawn', an old Norse tune associated with gaiety and festivity.
Invariably the fiddler was treated to a dram, and before he had
finished his round his playing ability was considerably im-
paired. The laird of Busta once had on his estate a blind fiddler
with a large family, to whom he gave a croft and house rent
free on condition that he woke the laird on Yule morning
playing 'Da Day Dawn' on the stairhead of his manor house.

Yule Day was invariably wound up with a rant which continued until midnight. On this occasion the favourite reel tune
was 'Da Foula Reel', another tune expressive of the Shetland
character. Words were set to it, the first verse running as
follows:

> Weel since we are welcome tae Yule, up wi't lightfoot
>   link it awa boys
> Send for a fiddler play up Foula reel, we'll skip as light as
>   a maa boys.
> *Chorus*
> Da Shaalds o Foula will pay for a', up wi't lightfoot link
>   it awa boys
> Da Shaalds o Foula will pay for a', da Shaalds will pay for
>   a' boys.

The Shaalds are fishing grounds near the island of Foula and
the message on Yule Night was one of eat, drink and be merry
with no thought of the morrow. On this one night of the year

they were able to set their fears aside in the belief that the next year's fishing would solve all their problems.

In 1867 John Reid, the artist, described a custom that was observed in some places on 10th January, the last night of the old year. A group of five lads consisting of a 'gentleman' and a 'carrying horse' and three others all disguised would go from house to house singing what they called a New Year's Even's Sang and collecting provisions for a banquet on New Year's Night. The 'gentleman' wore a cap made of straw with his name on the front, a collar of straw around his neck, a belt of straw around his waist and a band of straw around his right arm. His duty was to sing the song outside the door, and when he had finished he would enter the house and introduce himself as Vanderigan come from Dronton (Trondheim). The song itself was obviously a relic of Roman Catholic times, the phrase 'Saint Mary's men are we' being repeated in each verse. Reid assumed that it was probably sung originally by monks on their New Year begging excursions.

On New Year's Day work of every kind was resumed. Men went fishing, girls resumed sewing and knitting, a few clods of earth were turned over and fishing gear was repaired. It was important to start the new year well with God's blessing on the work of the sea and land. But this was still not the end of the celebrations, for parties continued until 24th night on 29th January (O.S.), also known as Up-Helly-Aa, or the end of the holidays. This was marked by a party to end all parties in the house of someone with a large barn for dancing.

When John Reid made his tour of Shetland many of the old customs were becoming forgotten, and the process was to be quickened during the next few decades. One of the greatest factors in the decline of these customs was the adoption of the new calendar and a gradual change to the new style of Christmas as it was celebrated elsewhere in the U.K. The new style was introduced at Lerwick in 1879 and spread gradually to all parts of the islands. In 1886 it had been introduced to the parish of Delting, while in 1894 it was celebrated at Mid Yell, Aywick, and Westsandwick for the first time. But there was no sudden break with the old calendar, for in most places many people refused to conform and celebrated their own festival eleven days later.

Before the end of the century, however, many of the old customs had died out, and their decline can be seen from the reports of rural correspondents in the local newspapers. In 1896 it was reported in *The Shetland News* that in North Yell football was not so popular on Yule Day, while the Fetlar correspondent noted that there was 'not the usual turnout on the football field'. At Haroldswick it was observed that 'out of door sports such as football on Xmas Day and New Year's Day seem to be declining here'. The following year at Delting football was played on both Old Christmas and Old New Year's Day, but in 1898 the Weisdale correspondent reported sadly: 'Kicking the ba' seems to be a thing of the past'. Mr Peter Moar of Lerwick remembers the game of doors being played for the last time at Westing, Unst on old Christmas Day 1900 (or perhaps 1901) and this is perhaps the last occasion when it was played anywhere in Shetland.

The custom of soliciting food on New Year's Eve continued for half a century after John Reid described it. It survived in parts of the west side of Shetland in the form of Huggeranoh-ni, when two or more boys carrying pillowcases tied to a length of wood went from house to house gathering oranges, apples, gingerbread and other dainties. This custom was still being observed at Skeld between the wars, as told by John R. Cheyne in *The New Shetlander*.

Although shorn of much of their former glory, the observance of old Christmas on 5th January and old New'r'day a week later survived even longer, as in most parts of Shetland there developed an intermediate step with two sets of festivals. Some places such as Papa Stour actually resisted the introduction of the new style until between the wars. Before long most parts of Shetland observed Christmas by the new calendar but held another celebration a week later, partly to honour tradition, partly as an excuse for an extra celebration. The last place to do so is the island of Foula, and there is every indication that the double set of festivals will continue for several years yet.

OLD YULE AT LERWICK

Throughout most of the nineteenth century Christmas was celebrated by the people of Lerwick in their own unique way.

Christmas Eve began quietly enough with the arrival in the streets of da peerie guizers, the children of the town all wearing fancy dress and going the rounds of the shops and houses soliciting coppers from their elders. They were replaced towards midnight by the older guizers, arranged in groups or squads, waiting impatiently for the night's fun to begin.

As soon as the bell of the Tolbooth sounded the last stroke of midnight the whole town erupted in a fusillade of pistol shots and the firing of seven- and twelve-pound guns. At that time gunpowder could be obtained in every general merchant's shop, since muzzle loading guns were common, and even those who possessed breech loaders filled their own cartridges. A real pistol could be bought for little more than five shillings, and many hundreds of strong dependable weapons made by local experts were in existence and sold for under a shilling each.

It has been suggested that this obsession with gunpowder dates from the period of wars at the beginning of the eighteenth century when the fort at Lerwick was garrisoned, the harbour was full of armed, navy vessels, the streets were crowded with soldiers and seamen and literally thousands of Shetland men were serving in the Royal Navy where they themselves became acquainted with firearms. When peace came in 1815 there were nationwide celebrations, and in Lerwick the newly demobbed seamen sought to make it a day to remember.

From then on it seems that the young men of Lerwick vied with each other in developing new ways of celebrating Christmas. It had to be observed with ostentation and noise and within a few years Lerwick had the reputation of having the most boisterous type of Christmas celebration in the whole of Europe.

A feature of the period was the growing popularity of the tar barrel. The name is misleading since a tar barrel was actually a heavy wooden sledge bearing between four and ten tubs filled with old rope, wood chips and a plentiful supply of tar all blazing furiously. This was dragged up and down Lerwick's narrow lanes and back and forth along Commercial Street until the squad in charge decided it was time to let the tar barrel burn itself out on one of the stone piers that then fringed the shoreline of Lerwick.

Although constructed in secrecy by a single squad of six or eight guizers, the members of other squads joined in whenever required to drag the heavy contraption along. At least two members of the squad wore sacks over their heads to save them from blobs of molten tar, since their job was to stir the contents of the tubs with long wooden poles. Flames leaped as high as the rooftops and doors and windows were frequently blistered with the heat. The number of tar barrels depended on the ability of a squad to 'acquire' the material required and keep it hidden from the police. On a typical Yule morning at least three were bound to make their appearance.

After the burning of the tar barrels the squads of guizers went their separate ways in a round of the houses that remained open to receive them. There they were entertained to refreshments and danced with the young ladies who had gathered for that purpose. It was considered the duty of each squad to visit as many houses as possible, and this part of the morning's proceedings lasted until nine a.m. or later. These activities—the burning of tar barrels and visiting of houses by the various squads—were repeated on New Year's morning and at Up-Helly-Aa.

It is not surprising that the authorities tried to suppress the tar barrels. Each Christmas a body of forty or fifty special constables were sworn in to assist the Chief of Police and seize the tar barrels as soon as they made their appearance on the Hillhead. Sometimes they were successful in dragging the burning device to a spot where it could be overturned and allowed to burn out harmlessly, but at other times, when the sledge was bowling along with considerable momentum, they could do nothing more than run alongside with the crowd until the planned burning site was reached. On the whole the attention of the specials did little more than give the custom an added attraction, as the squad did their best to outwit them.

There are many stories told of tar barrels being dragged down narrow lanes with the specials in pursuit, many of them ex-tar barrellers themselves and sympathetic to the boys. There are tales of hand-to-hand fights watched by a crowd of revellers and accompanied by pistol and cannon shots. On one occasion the specials were actually locked in the Tolbooth and not liberated until half past seven in the morning, by which time the last of the morning's tar barrels had been successfully burned beside the Cockstool Rock just below the Tolbooth. However, the authorities triumphed in the end. Tar barrelling was getting out of hand, and a great deal of damage to public property was now an accepted part of the Yule festivities, so a law banning the burning of tar barrels was passed in 1874.

In place of the tar barrels came a more sedate torchlight procession which continued for a few years until this entire aspect of Old Christmas was incorporated in the reorganized festival of Up-Helly-Aa.

UP-HELLY-AA

In all parts of Shetland the prolonged festivities of Yule were brought to a close with 24th night or Up-Helly-Aa on 29th January. According to Mrs. Saxby some young people clubbed together and spent the evening dancing, while others disguised as grüliks formed a procession and marched through the township with lighted torches which at midnight were piled with other combustible material into a huge bonfire. In Lerwick Up-Helly-Aa was a night for burning tar barrels and for guizing, although to some respects it was less important than Christmas or New Year's morning. All this was to change, however, after the banning of tar barrels in 1874.

The torchlight procession inaugurated in 1876 continued for a few years as an important feature of the Christmas celebrations, then in 1881 it was switched to the night of Up-Helly-Aa. For a time it seemed that the whole tradition of guizing and entertaining guizers was about to disappear, and indeed in 1883 there was not a single house open to receive them. The festival continued in a desultory fashion for the rest of the decade, then in 1889 an innovation appeared in the form of a model Viking longship which was dragged along the streets as part of the procession before being burned at the Market Cross.

It was clear that a movement was afoot to re-introduce into Up-Helly-Aa some of the old Norse associations, and this trend was to become accentuated in the 1890s. Eighteen ninety-five saw the introduction of organized singing with the rousing words of 'The Hardy Norseman'—a song that glorified the deeds of the old Vikings. During the burning of the galley, however, the crowd sang the typically Scottish song—'Auld Lang Syne'.

In 1897 a new song was written specially for Up-Helly-Aa by James J. Haldane Burgess, the poet and author who did more than anyone to keep alive Shetland's Norse traditions. It was known as the Up-Helly-Aa song and, set to music by Mr Thomas Manson, was immediately incorporated into the festival, being sung as the procession moved off. Again it glorifies the deeds of the old Vikings, and its opening verse stresses the links between the festival and the Shetlanders' Norse forebears.

> From grand old Viking centuries Up-Helly-Aa has come,
> Then light the torch and form the march and sound the rolling
>   drum.
> Awake the mighty memories of heroes that are dumb;
> The waves are rolling on.

In 1935 the guizers acquired yet another song known as 'The Galley Song', written by the author John Nicolson and set to a stirring tune adapted from an old Norwegian folk song. There were now three songs associated with Up-Helly-Aa—the Up-Helly-Aa Song itself sung as the procession started, 'The Galley Song' which preceded the burning of the galley and 'The Norseman's Home' sung when the galley was well ablaze. And with these songs the festival had assumed the basic structure which still continues to the present day—the greatest spectacle in the island year.

The Cycle of Life

Nowadays most confinements take place in the maternity wing of the Gilbert Bain hospital, and it is salutary to reflect on the conditions in which children were born a century ago, when there was neither doctor nor nurse in attendance, but only a howdie or midwife who had learned her trade from a well-meaning but equally unskilled older woman. At that time there were no pain-killing drugs nor gas/air mixture to ease the pains of childbirth, but at best a Bible and an open razor to scare the trows away. Even when superstitious beliefs began to lessen their hold, there was no corresponding improvement in medical care, and it goes without saying that infant mortality was high and that many mothers died of childbed fever.

It is not surprising that the safe delivery of a healthy baby was a cause of great celebration, not only among the members of the family but among the entire community. There were no less than three feasts or celebrations associated with birth—the Blithe Feast after the child was born, when the women of the neighbourhood called to congratulate the mother; the Fittin Feast when the mother came back and resumed her duties around the fire; and the Christening after the baby had been taken to the Church and baptized.

In spite of the relative poverty of the islands childhood was generally a happy time. Even though the mother might be out working in the fields, there was always someone to croon over a fractious bairn and to rock it to sleep—perhaps an older sister, a grandmother or even a poor old 'quarter' wife who was maintained by each house in the district in turn.

Shetland children were never banished to spend long lonely

hours in a nursery in the care of a stranger. From their earliest days they were part of an overcrowded household usually incorporating three or more generations, and their nursery was the but end where there was always plenty of people to play with them, fondle them in their arms and dance them on their knees. Their first awareness of their own bodies came through the rhymes of an adult, their fingers and toes being pointed out as the following lines were recited:

> Diss is da een at brook da barn,
> Diss is da een at stöl da coarn,
> Diss is da een at ran awa,
> Diss is da een at telled aa,
> An diss is da een at fell ida gutter an peyed for aa.

The parts of the child's head figured in this verse, being indicated by an older person's finger.

> Chin chin cherry,
> Mooth mooth merry,
> Nose nose nappie,
> Eye eye blinkie,
> Brow brow brackie
> An awa ower da tappie.

And if a child refused to eat its food the mother would seat it in her lap and go through the following routine with her left hand while she held the spoon in her right.

> Knock on da door [forehead]
> Peep in [lift an eyelid]
> Lift da latch [touch the nose]
> An walk in [put the spoon into the mouth].

In its earliest days the child was left largely in the care of women. Father was a person who was away for long periods, but when he came home at the weekend or at the end of the fishing or whaling season he would spend hours with his son or daughter, lift it on to his knees and bounce it up and down as if it were on horseback, reciting a poem such as:

Upride upride upride da bairn,
Ride awa ride awa ride awa da njuggle,
Haud de tongue, cuddle doon,
An du sall gyit a bogel.

Then when tired out after its boisterous playtime the child would be handed over to its grandmother, who would lay its head on her breast and hush it to sleep, perhaps reciting:

Hushie baa, Minnie's daaty,
We sall pit da trows awa.
Broonie sanna gyit da bairn,
If he comes da cocks'll craa.

Two facts instilled into the child from its earliest days were the need to respect the unknown creatures in the world outside and yet the safety of home.

There was a great deal to interest the child growing up on a croft in the crops and the animals, and its earliest journeys from the house were taken with its mother when she went to flit da kye or went to the rig for a denner o' tatties. Its earliest toys were cows and sheep—not the perfect toy farm animals, but substitutes found locally. The dry skulls of ling and cod were cattle and the shells of the blue mussel were sheep, while whelks and buckies were hens and geese. More elaborate toys were made by their father or uncles—tiny wooden boats, models of tushkars and spades and little men that rocked to and fro when pivoted on the back of a chair, while a universal favourite was the dunderspell, a piece of wood with notched sides that made a roaring noise when tied to a piece of string and whirled around the head. And when they lost interest in these they could make their own toys like the snorrie benn, a special bone in the foot of a pig which was fastened to a length of string and when a loop was held in each hand it could be made to whir as the string was alternately relaxed and tightened. Another easily made toy was the windy craa—simply a potato stuck all over with hens' feathers—whose antics on a windy day never failed to amuse a child.

In the cramped space of the but end only quiet games were possible—those that required little room. A favourite was 'Row da boats o' Maeli', in which two children sat on the floor facing each other with their legs outstretched. After leaning forward to take hold of each other's hands they commenced to 'row' backwards and forwards, reciting as they did so:

> Row da boats o' Maeli,
> Ship inunder saili,
> Row stoot, row strong,
> Brak da boats at winna come on.

At the word 'brak' each tried to be the first to loosen his grip and make the other fall flat on his back.

Another favourite was called 'stealin swine'. It was played all over Shetland and there are many different versions including one spoken in Norn. The following version is one of those from Unst recorded by Mrs Jessie M. E. Saxby. One player sat on a stool with a cloth in his hand, and before him on the floor he placed from four to six medium sized potatoes. The second player then approached and recited:

> I'm come fae da high laands
> Gyain tae da lowlands
> Seekin swine, geese an gaeslins.
> We lost a peerie aalie pootie
> An me midder sent me ta see
> If he wis among your eens.

'Look you, you're welcome,' the seated player replied. Then the other began to lift and examine each potato in turn remarking 'It's no dis een, it's no dis een'. The aim of the game was to get one into his hand and escape before the seated player could touch him with his cloth. If touched he had to replace the potato and go through the procedure again. When successful, the players changed places.

Children started school at a much later age than they do nowadays. There was no bus or car waiting for them each morning—in fact there was seldom a road to follow, but merely a footpath over the hills. When the little thatched schoolroom was several miles away children seldom commenced their education before the age of six or seven, and attendance generally continued only until the age of twelve, by which time the child was expected to pull his or her weight at home. Many boys worked on the drying beaches from May to August and resumed their studies during winter. Teachers were rarely qualified and the curriculum was confined to the three Rs and the catechism, with a little navigation for those boys who could benefit from it. Nevertheless some of the schoolmasters played a valuable part in improving the life of the whole district—men like John Peterson at Skerries, John Turnbull Smith at Scalloway and Robert Jamieson at Sandness.

The Education Act of 1872 was as much a watershed in Shetland as it was elsewhere. It made education compulsory and saw the erection of vastly improved school buildings, although such refinements as school transport were still almost a century away. Instead of having a hot meal at midday children were turned out into the playground to make the most of a brünnie and a bottle of milk or other food brought with them from home. Lunch over, they passed the rest of the midday break playing games such as King Kumalay, Hyste da Flag, Cripple Kirsie, Foo money miles ta Babylon, many of these remembered now only in name.

And when the long school day was over it was back to the croft and the familiar faces, the crops, the animals and the household chores reserved for the children of the family. There was no weekend job to bring them a little pocket money but there was the seashore, and many a shilling was earned by gathering winkles at low tide, storing them in a sack placed just above low water mark until they had collected a sufficient quantity to sell to the local merchant.

It was not all work, for they had more games to play, such as hedderkindunk (see-saw), pickie and follow da leader, while on moonlight nights in autumn they played skoitamillyaskroo —a form of hide and seek among the skroos of corn in the yard.

For girls life soon assumed the more humdrum pattern that characterized their lives—a monotonous round of baking and cleaning, of fetching and carrying, of caring for the very young and learning to fill even their moments of leisure by cairding, spinning and knitting.

For boys life was far more interesting. Fish had to be caught either from a boat or from the rocks, and while it was certainly an important occupation it was also a source of enjoyment.

When autumn spates filled the burns there were sea-trout to be caught in a hoovie—a trap constructed at one time from long straight stocks of docken, and laterally made of net woven on to two stout pieces of wood. The hoovie was set; then, armed with long poles which had clumps of heather on the ends the boys would go upstream and scare the fish down towards the trap.

During periods of bad weather when the wind was blowing straight onshore, exposing the beaches to the full reach of the Atlantic or the North Sea, every able-bodied man maintained a constant patrol during hours of daylight to make certain of his share of the driftwood, barrels and boxes that the sea might cast up. This too was considered work fit for a boy, and a healthy, invigorating job it was, too, full of interest and excitement, for one never knew what to expect from one day to the next. It was on such occasions that they learned that the sea is not to be trifled with, since all too often among the broken timbers of ships were the bodies of drowned seamen.

When hairst brought a relaxation to the work of the croft and the darkening nights afforded protection, the boys sallied forth on their favourite early winter pastime of playing tricks on their elders. These activities reached their peak at Hallowe'en. A common prank was to climb on to the roof of a neighbouring house and place a poan or other obstruction over the lum or chimney, then watch from a safe distance the antics of the occupants as they rushed out coughing and spluttering. Another common prank usually reserved for Hallowe'en was to drop a cabbage through the roof opening. It was disconcerting for the family when, just as the supper pot on the links was coming to the boil, a large cabbage, roots, earth and all, would splash into it, scattering the contents. More harmless forms of amusement were tying doors from the outside so that they could not be opened until the boys relented.

Of course, the occupants of the house invariably gave chase, and if caught the boys were unceremoniously thrashed, but later, when the mess had been cleared away, the victims of the prank would laugh and confess that the lads were merely doing what each generation of boys had done for hundreds of years, and that if they had failed to carry on the tradition the criticism would have been levelled at them that boys were not what they used to be.

For young people in general winter was the season for social gatherings, especially cairdings, when the young women were invited to each house in rotation to prepare a stock of wool for spinning. With aprons protecting their clothes they worked away with a break for tea at eight o'clock. Then about nine or ten the young men would drop in to chat and joke with the lasses. Finally the wool and the aprons were laid aside, the fiddle was taken down off the shelf and the floor was cleared for dancing. Generally it was three or four in the morning before the company dispersed, and for those whose homes were several miles away a lang bed or shakedown of straw and blankets was made up in the barn, and the young men and women lay down together and slept till breakfast time.

Interspersed with the cairdings were rants or dances usually held in the largest barn in the district. The earthen floor was swept as clean as the bussom could make it, the flails were laid away and a dozen or more sheaves—perhaps those destined for the cattle's morning feed—were piled up in one corner as the seat of honour for the fiddler. Again at the end of the dance a lang bed was made up on the floor for those whose homes lay some distance away.

In other parts of the United Kingdom it is said that spring is the time for affairs of the heart, but in Shetland this was seldom the case. Spring was the time for fitting out the boats and preparing for the summer fishing season, but in autumn and winter there was more time for romance.

Courtship was a secret affair, and it was exceptional for a young man to be seen out with his girl unless at a wedding. It was partly the need for secrecy that gave rise to the custom known outside Shetland as bundling, whereby the pair of lovers were permitted to spend the night together in the girl's bed lying fully dressed in each other's arms. Inevitably the custom was much criticized by visitors to these islands, who imagined that it would result in immorality. But although exceptions did occur, it seems that in the vast majority of cases it was done in an atmosphere of innocence that seems incredible to people living in the so-called permissive society of today. This pattern of courtship was once common in several parts of Northern

Europe, made necessary by the rigours of the climate and the lack of privacy in the small overcrowded houses of the period.

It was not long before everyone knew that young Robbie o' da Pund and John Tamson's Mary were gyaain trang taegidder. Yet marriage might be delayed for years while the young man went to sea in order to save enough money to enable them to set up house. In spite of long periods of separation it was unthinkable for the girl to befriend any other man. Indeed there were cases where a young man was lost at sea and his girl went into mourning and continued to wear sombre black for the rest of her days.

But in most cases the young man came home to marry, and again this was an occasion generally reserved for the winter season. There was no formal asking for the hand of the girl in marriage but a well-established pattern nevertheless, with the presentation of a bottle of gin or brandy—da spuirin bottle— to the girl's father.

Dressed in his best clothes the young man, striving hard to hide his embarrassment, would make for his girl friend's house. He would be welcomed at the fireside by the family, who would suspect immediately the reason for his visit. After a cup of tea, during which the topic of conversation was usually as far removed as possible from the business in hand, the young man would produce the bottle and ask for a wine glass to be brought to him. The reception given to the dram was the answer to the young man's unspoken request. In fact it was almost unknown for the suitor to be turned down. Having been encouraged so far, it was certain that he was considered a suitable candidate for the hand of the daughter of the house.

The Saturday after the spuirin was known as Contract Saturday, when the bride-to-be invited her friends and neighbours including the groom and his family to her parents' house to settle the 'contract'. The guests were entertained to a sumptuous meal, a fat sheep having been killed for the occasion. Next day the couple were proclaimed in church for the first time, this being repeated a week later.

Then came the preparations for the wedding, to which the whole community were usually invited, the groom and his best man going from house to house and bidding the people by word of mouth. Thursday used to be the most popular day for weddings and it was important that the day coincided with a new or growing moon to ensure good luck. Early in the week the couple with the best man and bridesmaid took their way to Lerwick to procure the bride's trousseau, the bridesmaid's dress and other necessities. In some cases it was a long journey on foot, and it often involved remaining in town overnight, staying with relatives.

The day before the wedding was spent in preparations as the women of the bride's family and their friends were busy baking bread, the men were slaughtering sheep for the feast while the young girls of the community put the finishing touches to their hats and dresses.

It is clear that the traditional Shetland wedding was a momentous occasion, as elaborate as the two families' resources stretched to the full could make it. There was no standard pattern and there was such variation from place to place that it is now possible only to compile a composite picture from a number of sources. The wedding day usually started with the men assembling at the groom's house for breakfast while the young women gathered at the house of the bride's parents. Breakfast over, the men set off for the bride's house, where they formed a line a short distance from the door. Three shots were fired, and on the third the door opened and the bride walked out with her maidens towards the waiting males, taking care to make a half-circle towards the left, or going sungaets—the path that always led to good fortune. After kissing every man present, each girl paired off with her partner who would walk, dance and eat with her during the wedding.

Then the march to church began, accompanied by one or more fiddlers and headed by two older married people known as 'da honest folk'. Next came the bridegroom and best maid, then the bride walking with the best man and finally the guests, with the bride's youngest sister and the groom's youngest brother at the rear.

After the wedding ceremony, which was performed either in the church or in the manse, the procession re-assembled for the march back to the house of the bride's parents. There was a change in the order of the procession, since it was now headed by the newly wedding pair, followed by the best man and bridesmaid and the honest folk in third place. Men with shotguns walked alongside firing shots into the air as rapidly as the guns could be reloaded.

As the procession neared the house they were met by an old woman carrying in a clean white cambric napkin oatcakes broken into small pieces. This was known as the bride's bonn or blessing and it was thrown over the heads of the company. There followed a scramble to catch a piece of the bonn, since if put under one's pillow it would ensure pleasant dreams and good fortune. It was only a simple piece of plain oatcake, but great importance was attached to it. It must be remembered that bread was not taken for granted in the way it is today. The children of the neighbourhood also gathered around the house demanding, and invariably receiving, money to buy the traditional ba.

The arrangements for the wedding reception depended on the layout and the available space of the house itself. In most cases the but end with the furniture removed was laid out with boards and trestles and wooden seats for the meal while dancing went on in the barn or the ben end. The meal was described in great detail by Peter Jamieson in his book *The Viking Isles*:

> All being seated the bride's piece was served first, then began the bridal feast of great steaming dishes of boiled mutton chopped into fine bits. This was da stov, or meat from the carcases of sheep gifted as wedding presents. Then roasted mutton, beef, pork, salt fish, oatmeal cakes, burstane cakes, flour meal bannocks, bere meal brünnies, butter, kirn mylk, brose, sheep's heads, puddings, ale, tea, whisky, wine and the rest followed, the feast going ahead in right royal fashion, for as the Shetlanders say 'hit's no every nicht at Marta mairries'.

A feature of the wedding dance was the arrival of the guizers —young men dressed in fantastic suits of straw, ornamented with coloured ribbons. The leader who entered first was known as the skudler and his face was usually covered with a white napkin, while on his head he wore a straw cap with three loops at the top from which coloured ribbons hung down so as to almost cover the cap. The moment he entered the room he made a strange snoring sound and performed a dance, then he was joined by another guizer known as the gentleman, by a third known as the fool and finally by three more. The six were careful not to reveal their identity, and when they finally took their leave they usually left behind them a generous gift for the bride.

After this interruption dancing was resumed, and continued until it was time to sit down to breakfast, after which the company dispersed, promising to return for the second night. In this way some weddings 'stood' for up to three days, depending on the means of the families concerned,

When starting married life together few couples were blessed with an abundance of material possessions. Indeed some set up house with little more than a couple of spades, a tushkar and a cow in the byre, while the girl usually brought with her from her parents' house her spinning wheel and her wooden chair. This set the scene for the spartan life of hard work and raising a large family—families of ten or more were by no means uncommon, although it was seldom that all of them reached adulthood. For the husband it was a life of crofting and fishing as previous generations had experienced for hundreds of years —an existence in which death by drowning came to be accepted as a way of life.

Whenever the husband was lost an added burden fell on the widow, since she had to become breadwinner as well as mother and housewife. In many cases she had her husband's debts to settle before she could start her new task, and there is at least one recorded case of a merchant coming to a widow's house and removing a cow from the byre to settle her husband's account. Food was the main priority, and in some cases a woman had to start her day by going to the craigseats to catch a few sillocks to boil for her family's breakfast. Of course in most cases the deceased's brothers and sisters, and those of the widow too, did their best to assist the bereaved family, bringing up some of the children as their own if necessary.

Even when the husband survived a woman's life was far from easy, since for long periods during the growing season she was left in charge of the crops and livestock. Women were often old before their time, their backs bent from years of toil and carrying heavy loads in their kishies.

Men and women who lived to a ripe old age were the lucky ones, those who saw their children grow up and marry with

another generation of children running around the but end fire.
A grandmother was often given the name Minnie, while a grand-
father was usually known as Da—terms of respect as befitted
a lifetime of experience and the wisdom that their years had
conferred on them.

For old men life came full circle with a return to some of
the pursuits they had enjoyed as boys. Dr Hibbert realized this
when he wrote in 1817:

> While active manhood is left at liberty to follow the more labori-
> ous occupations of the deep water fishery and to navigate the
> Greeland seas, it is to the sinewless arm of youth or to the
> relaxed fibres of old age that the light task is resigned of wielding
> the sillock rod.

Inevitably age brought its own disadvantages, and the crip-
pling pains of rheumatism confined many old people for long
periods to the fireside or to their beds. When they became a
burden and required more patience and more attention than the
hard working family could readily afford, the younger generation would excuse the cantankerous moods of the elderly with
the remark: 'Aald folk is twise bairns'.

Death brought its own three ceremonies—da kistin, when
the body was laid in the coffin, da condolin when the neighbours came to offer their sympathy and the funeral itself,
which was accompanied by a range of customs that showed
considerable variation throughout Shetland and altered with
the years. George Low records that in Unst when a funeral procession passed by the bystanders threw lumps of earth after
the corpse. Dr Hibbert related how a plate of salt was placed
on top of the corpse as it lay in the coffin, and John R. Tudor
referred to the practice of burning the straw of the deathbed—
da leek strae—soon after the coffin was removed from the
house. It was the custom to examine the ashes left in the belief
that there would be seen the footprints of the next person to
die in that neighbourhood.

In most cases the coffin was placed outside the house on a
couple of chairs, and when lifted at the start of the slow procession to the churchyard the chairs had to be kicked over,
otherwise, or so it was believed, they would soon be required

for that purpose again. The coffin was carried by teams of pall bearers in relays, and the bereaved family was expected to provide an ample supply of whisky to refresh the mourners on the way. Whether the deceased had been rich or poor the men of the community turned out in force to show their last respects. Mere wealth was never a true indication of a person's standing in the community.

II

The Dawn of Modern Times

The Crofters Holdings (Scotland) Acts of 1886 have been called the 'Crofters' Magna Carta', since with a stroke of the pen the crofters were granted security of tenure, the right to a fair negotiated rent and compensation for improvement carried out during their tenancy. No longer could the landlord use the threat of eviction to make the crofter subservient to his will.

This new-found freedom was soon put to the test when on 14th September 1888 over 300 whales were driven ashore on the beach at Hoswick, and the two landlords demanded their third of the proceeds as usual. The fishermen refused and the case was taken to Lerwick Sheriff Court, where after considering the evidence Sheriff MacKenzie found that the landowners had no right to any share of the proceeds.

Unwilling to admit defeat, the landowners next took their case to the Court of Session in Edinburgh, where the fishermen feared a different verdict would result. A fund was established to help the fishermen in their legal battle, contributions coming from Shetland exiles in all parts of Britain and overseas. But their fears were groundless, for the Court of Session upheld the decision of Sheriff MacKenzie that henceforth the proceeds from whale hunts should go to the crofters alone.

There was no backlash against the landlords for their years of oppression, although resentment in the southern part of Shetland culminated in the Cunningsburgh disturbances of 1890 and 1891, triggered off by a barbed wire fence across the Clift Hills which it was claimed was damaging the crofters' sheep. Again the people were victorious and the offending fence was removed.

Eighteen ninety saw the first election for the newly constituted Zetland County Council, and there was considerable dis-
quiet in the northern part of Dunrossness when it was discovered that the voters in Dunrossness South had returned as their
member Mr John Bruce, an able and intelligent man, but as
local landowner, and indeed one of the two involved in the
Hoswick Whale Case, he was symbolic of the old age of oppression. As a result of this the herring fishermen of Levenwick declared a boycott on the line fishermen of South Dunrossness,
refusing to provide them with their customary supply of herring
as bait.

Generally speaking, laird and tenant got down together quietly to the task of reorganizing the crofting system. The Crofters'
Commission began their sittings in Shetland in August 1889,
and after listening to the appeals of crofters rents were generally reduced by about a quarter. But mere legislation could
not overcome the basic problems affecting Shetland's agriculture—the smallness of the crofts, remoteness from markets
and, above all, the difficulties posed by the climate.

Eighteen ninety-two was a disastrous year, with a wretched
spring and summer, and many people had no seed for the following season. Relief grants were voted by the government for the
North-West Highlands and Islands to provide seed oats, and
these were later extended to finance the construction of roads
and footpaths. The Society of Friends again provided valuable
assistance by donating 177 quarters of seed for distribution
among 589 needy crofters in Unst, Yell and Fetlar. Eighteen
ninety-four, on the other hand, was one of the best years ever
known in Shetland, and the corn was cut and in the yard before the end of September.

The enquiries into crofting conditions made at the end of
the nineteenth century resulted in a large amount of information regarding the economics of the industry. The Crofters'
Commission was told that a typical croft with three acres of
arable land would yield 56 bushels of oats, between 80 and 150
ankers of potatoes besides cabbages and turnips. The outrun
and hill pasture together would support three Shetland cows
and three younger animals, one or two ponies, a pig and about
twenty sheep. From the livestock a quey and cow sold each
year would realize seven pounds, while five sheep sold yearly

at eight shillings each would bring in two pounds. Such a croft would also have about thirty pounds of wool to dispose of at a shilling a pound. Added together, the annual income of this typical croft was fourteen pounds, while the fishing branch of the economy could be expected to bring in between seventeen and thirty pounds for the year. It is not surprising that many people sought a new life overseas, while those that remained often had to supplement the family's income by taking a job in the Merchant Navy.

No part of Shetland suffered more than Fair Isle did in the 1890s. The main export of the island was dried saithe, but the price remained at such a low level that it could hardly repay the trouble of catching and curing the fish. In the summer of 1897 no less than five families or about fifty people left the island to seek an improved living in Orkney and in Edinburgh.

Another problem in Fair Isle had arisen unexpectedly when the island's two lighthouses were erected in 1892. Although they made navigation in the area safer, the islanders claimed that ships no longer passed close by the island, and that this severely reduced the island's opportunity for trade.

This contention was not taken seriously by the rest of Shetland until September, 1897, when disaster struck the tiny community. A large number of sailing ships were spotted far out to the east of the island, and since the weather was fair four boats set off immediately to sell knitwear, eggs and vegetables. But before long the weather had worsened, and by nightfall only two of the boats had returned. Next morning another of the boats was spotted on the horizon and help was quickly on its way. But of the seven men on board four had died from exposure. The fourth boat with four men on board was never seen again.

IMPROVED LIVING STANDARDS

The most obvious of the changes that took place at the end of the nineteenth century was an improvement in living conditions. In some cases security of tenure acted as an incentive for tenants to carry out modest improvements themselves, but in most cases the changes were brought about by the County Council as it sought to implement the various Public Health Acts.

At this time new ideas were afoot concerning health and

sanitation, and the old croft houses once considered so convenient failed to meet the new requirements. Sanitary inspectors pointed out that the lack of light and inadequate ventilation were bad for the health of the occupants, while in most cases the houses were far too close to the byre and the midden.

In most places the thatched roofs were ripped off, being replaced with wooden roofs covered either with felt or slates. Many families took the opportunity of raising the walls during the operation and adding two little bedrooms upstairs under a coom ceiling. Doors were taken out in the front wall, often sheltered by a neat porch, and in most cases the door that connected house and byre was blocked.

Improvements came to the but end as the earthen floors were replaced by floors of wood and the fireplace was moved to a gable wall, where a proper chimney removed the problem of smoke. And improvements came to the ben end, too, with the dismantling of the box beds.

The reports of the sanitary inspectors and of the medical officers give a clear indication of the pace of these developments. By 1895 it was stated that more than two thirds of the houses in North Yell had wooden roofs, many of them covered with slate. In 1900 the medical report for Unst stated:

> The old thatched inconvenient houses are rapidly giving way to neat houses roofed with wood, covered with either tarred felt or canvas . . . Box beds are not nearly so common as they used to be, though for convenience the beds are built around the sides of the rooms. They are for the most part entirely open at one side and allow of being properly cleaned and ventilated.

In some cases, however, the people were reluctant to change, and in 1894 the County Council raised a test case to discover how far their statutory powers enabled them to deal with the many inadequate dwellings that still remained. They selected for their case a house at Hayknoll in Walls, which was an example of the old type of house without windows or chimneys and absolutely devoid of drainage, so that it was constantly damp. Its occupant maintained that he had lived there for twenty-one years and had brought up seven children, none of whom had suffered any illness apart from whooping cough.

Nevertheless Sheriff Shennan found that the dwelling constituted a nuisance and ordered the occupant to have the byre removed from the front of the house.

Even Lerwick's record was far from bright, since some of the houses in the lanes to the west of Commercial Street were far from healthy, and outbreaks of typhoid fever were quite common. The sanitary condition of the crofting township of Sound caused a good deal of concern, and the sanitary inspector's report of 1896 described how some of the houses there were half underground, damp and very unhealthy. Some minor improvements were carried out by having middens removed, closing up wells and altering the flow of drains. There was added concern since much of Lerwick's milk supply came from the crofts of Sound. A new Public Health Act came into force on 1st January 1897, and this gave the local authorities increased powers. It brought new provisions relating to water supply and drainage and more stringent regulations with regard to milk supplies.

IMPROVED COMMUNICATIONS

Communications between Shetland and the Scottish Mainland improved very slowly during the latter half of the nineteenth century. The introduction of the West Side steamer in 1881 played a major role in the development of the fishing industry but the service was hindered by the lack of lighthouses which made conditions extremely difficult in winter time. At this time during the winter months there was only one direct sailing each week between Lerwick and Aberdeen, which severely hampered the development of the white fish industry.

Fortunately the new interest in Shetland on the part of the British government was not confined to crofting matters alone. In 1890 the Western Highlands and Islands Commission came north to study the problems affecting communications. They listened carefully to all the proposals put forward, including the need for more lighthouses, the need for an extra direct sailing between Lerwick and Aberdeen. Surprisingly, Shetland was granted nearly everything that had been requested, including lighthouses at Vaila, Hamnavoe, Muckle Roe, Hillswick and other places and the extra link with Aberdeen. One proposal that did not receive their support was the suggestion that a

railway line should be constructed between Lerwick and Scalloway.

Road building continued at a slow but steady pace, and gradually branch roads were constructed to all the main centres
of population. The roads were narrow and unsurfaced but they
were a great improvement on the hill-tracks that they replaced.
The Sandness correspondent writing in *The Shetland News* of
29th December 1894 of improvements there gives a clear indication of the effect on the community :

> The carrying home of the peats formerly done entirely by the
> people themselves with their ponies is now done largely by cart ...
> Carts and dog carts now pass daily up and down the road where
> in old times, the hardy native carrying peats from the hill used
> with difficulty to maintain a precarious footing by winding sim-
> monds around his rivlins.

The extension of the road network led to a cycling craze in
the late 1890s and the formation of Zetland Cycling Club in
1897. Then in September 1902 Shetland saw a motor car for
the first time when an eight-horse-power Argyll was sent north
from Glasgow for the purpose of demonstration. It was reported that it completed the journey from Lerwick to North Roe
in four hours 'in spite of a head wind'. This was half the time
taken by the ordinary horse-drawn carriage. By 1911 there
were a dozen cars on the Mainland of Shetland alone, most of
them available for hire.

For the people who lived in the smaller islands communications remained more difficult. A steamer had replaced sailing
vessels on the route between Lerwick and the North Isles as
early as 1868, but the people of Bressay, Burra, Fair Isle, Foula,
Papa Stour and the numerous other islands still had to depend
on small open boats propelled by oar and sail. Accidents were
by no means uncommon, and as late as April 1913 three Whalsay men were drowned crossing from Nesting to Whalsay with
the mails. Fortunately the next few decades saw the introduction of much safer motor launches, many of them with enclosed
cabins for passengers, on practically all of these inter-island
routes.

ECONOMIC LIFE

The herring fishery rose steadily in the early part of the present century, the peak year being 1905, when over one million barrels of herring were exported. But although earnings exceeded one million pounds, only a fraction of this remained in Shetland, since most of the boats that took part came from other parts of Britain. Changes had taken place in this industry too to which the crofter-fishermen were unable to adapt.

The industry was becoming increasingly capital intensive, a change that had become apparent in the mid-1890s with a trend towards bigger and better sailing drifters approximately seventy feet in length and with a steam-driven capstan to take much of the toil out of hauling the nets. Few crofter fishermen had sufficient capital to invest in improved vessels, and as their older boats became unfit they were not replaced. For a few years the larger sailing boats fished for herring with considerable success; then about 1900 came the coal-burning steam drifters, owned by syndicates in Lowestoft, Yarmouth and Aberdeen and later by full-time fishermen in Scottish East Coast ports. The steam drifter was independent of wind and tide, could go farther afield to seek the herring shoals and return to port first to secure the best price. The steam drifter came to dominate the industry, and the number of sailing boats declined even more drastically in the first decade of the twentieth century.

Salvation for some of the sailing boats came with the introduction of petrol-paraffin engines, the first being installed about 1910, and this gave a large roomy sailing boat a catching potential only slightly less than that of a steam drifter. Even this required an appreciable investment of capital which few of the part-time crofter-fishermen could afford. But in several parts of Shetland communities of full-time fishermen were becoming established, especially in Lerwick and Scalloway and in the islands of Whalsay, Skerries, and Burra. In the latter island the lovely little village of Hamnavoe developed purely as a fishing village, marking the complete separation of the two industries of crofting and fishing.

For the crofter there was no alternative employment in Shetland. The haaf fishing had gone, and so had the cod fishing at Faroe. There were generally three choices open to him—he could emigrate, he could take a job in the Merchant Navy and return home for part of the year, or he could stay and make the best of a way of life which could not provide the standard of living then taken for granted almost everywhere else in Britain. The fact that so many chose to remain shows the tenacity of the Shetland crofter and the hold that the traditional way of life had on many people.

The coming of the steam drifter was not solely to blame for the decline in the islands' herring industry. About 1907 the herring shoals seemed to alter their usual migratory movements, and thereafter they appeared in far smaller concentrations on West Side grounds. This resulted directly in the decline of all the smaller ports and the cessation of operations at Walls, Papa Stour, Ronas Voe, Hillswick, Whalfirth and eventually Cullivoe, while the most dramatic effect of all was seen at Baltasound. Lerwick alone escaped the depression of those years, and it actually rose in importance to become the major herring port in Scotland.

The winter haddock fishery continued to provide employment for many between October and March, but prices remained low, and in this branch of the industry too the effects of the industrial revolution were painfully evident. In the 1890s the rich fishing grounds around Shetland attracted the attention of steam trawlers from Aberdeen, Dundee, Granton and North Shields. In theory they were debarred by law from fishing within a narrow three-mile zone around the shores, but within this strip lay most of the haddock grounds and the three-mile limit became practically ignored. Convictions were secured but they had little effect, since the high prices obtained for fresh haddock at mainland ports compensated for the occasional confiscation of gear.

The effect on little crofting and fishing communities was catastrophic as the inshore grounds were swept clean. Some men tried to keep fishing by going farther afield to seek patches of ground that the trawlers had not destroyed, but the open haddock boat was not designed for fishing at any great distance from land, especially in winter time.

The Delting disaster of December 1900 epitomizes the struggle and the tragedy of those years. It was a fine morning and seven boats had put to sea, three of them proceeding to what was known as the North Ground, off the south-east corner of the island of Yell. About ten thirty a.m. a terrific gale sprang up and the men cut their lines and made for the shore. One boat reached the safety of Symbister, a second reached Bonidale in Lunnasting while a third found shelter at Skerries. Four boats and twenty-two men were lost that day, and in the townships of Swinister, Firth, Toft and Nashon there were fifteen widows and fifty-one fatherless children.

The first half of the twentieth century was an unhappy time for Shetland, marred by unemployment and depopulation and the tragic events of two world wars in which hundreds of Shetlanders died. Changes came to the crofting way of life as the old home-made implements and utensils were replaced by factory made substitutes. The growing popularity of the Oliver horse-drawn plough made earlier types redundant, although an old-fashioned Shetland wooden plough was still in use at Cunningsburgh in 1914 drawn by an ox and a Shetland work-horse.

A few old water mills continued in use in remote places like Papa Stour, but elsewhere it was found more convenient to buy flour and meal from the local shop. The outbreak of war in 1914 made people realize how dependent they had become on imported goods, and in some places the old mills were repaired just in case. Many of the old meat and fish dishes remained popular. Early in the Second World War when bacon was in short supply in England someone remembered hearing about a kind of 'mutton pork' which used to be prepared in Shetland. The matter was raised in the House of Commons and figured in newspaper articles, and Shetlanders smiled, because this was obviously reestit mutton which many of them still prepared and enjoyed.

The years that followed the end of the Second World War saw a great number of minor improvements all over Shetland. Houses were modernized with the addition of kitchens and bathrooms, water being piped from the nearest well. Horse drawn ploughs and carts were banished to the scrap heap as mechanization took over first of all in the form of the two-wheeled 'Iron Horse' and soon afterwards in the shape of four-wheeled tractors. But these improvements did nothing to stop depopulation. Few new jobs were created, and the population continued to drop until there were fewer than 18,000 people left in Shetland by 1961.

The next few years, however, saw the remarkable economic revival of the 1960s, with a revitalization of the islands' traditional industries. The fishing fleet was rebuilt and new processing plants ensured that most of the islands' catch of haddock and whiting could be filleted and frozen locally before shipment to market, thus saving on freight charges and providing much needed employment. New ideas were introduced to crofting and to the manufacture of knitwear. By 1971 the population was rising again, proving that the downward trend of a hundred years had been reversed. Then came the discovery of oil in the East Shetland Basin, and ironically it was realized that during all those centuries of struggle and hardship Shetlanders were sitting literally on the edge of some of the richest oilfields in the world.

Shetland's Heritage

The sea that has for so long isolated these islands has also insulated them to a great extent from outside influences, preserving a unique island culture that bears the mark of all the races that have influenced these islands in the last thousand years and more.

There is abundant evidence of the Norsemen who colonized Shetland in the eighth and nine centuries. Practically every place name comes straight from the Old Norse language, although it frequently requires a little effort to restore them to their original form. High up on the hill above Lunna there is a tiny loch known as Loomashun—originally *loomr tjorn*, or the lochan of the great northern diver. It just requires one of these birds to settle on the grey surface of the loch and we are taken back a thousand years to the unknown Norse colonist who was first captivated by the sight. Between Girlsta and Laxfirth there is a lonely croft known today as Vatster—a name whose meaning is not immediately clear until we remember that this was *vatn setter*, or the farm beside the lake. There are hundreds of examples where the old Norse name is still as appropriate as ever.

Unfortunately many beautiful old names were lost during the depopulation of the late nineteenth and early twentieth centuries. It was not merely that crofts became abandoned and fell into ruins—the rig names and names of heights and hollows used by generations of crofters became forgotten. In spite of the work of Dr Jakobsen and others of his generation there was little interest in preserving the old, apparently unimportant relics of the past, and when new houses were built they were invariably given modern English names such as 'Seaview', 'Primrose Cottage' or 'Roseville'. Even after the Second World War, postal addresses such as No. 1 New Houses or No. 2 Cruden became established. More recently, vigorous attempts have been made to preserve the old names, and council schemes have been given names such as Skelladale at Brae, Lingaro at Bixter and Hulsidale at Hamnavoe. At Sound near Lerwick, a Norwegian name was devised for the housing scheme of Sandveien —'the way to the Sand'.

In spite of all the changes of the last 100 years, the crofts remain the most attractive feature of the landscape. In most cases the houses have been modernized or replaced with attractive bungalows, and occasionally the old house becomes a store or a tractor shed. But the rigs still lie on the lower slopes, being turned over in voar by tractor or left lying green as pasture for sheep. Surprisingly, there are one or two relics of the run-rig system. At Sandness there is a meadow held in halvers, although it is many years since hay was last cut on it. At Tresta in Fetlar, four small meadow sections rotated annually among the four crofters concerned until 1955.

Sheep rearing is now an important part of crofting, and each crofter continues to have his own distinctive mark to identify his sheep on the scattald. In some places the fleeces are still rooed or removed by hand, although at most crøs the snick of the shears indicates that shearing is under way. Although the hills are still divided into scattalds, in some cases the greater proportion of the land has been apportioned or divided among the crofters concerned as a prelude to improvement by reseeding, thus enabling them to carry a far greater stock of sheep.

The skill of spinning wool by hand has been kept alive, but it is carried out mainly as a tourist attraction in summer time. Practically the entire wool clip is purchased by wool merchants and sent to the Scottish mainland, where it is spun by machine into yarn. It returns as hanks dyed in various colours by a chemical process.

From its humble beginnings as a purely cottage industry, knitting has developed into a major island industry. Traditional methods of manufacture could not keep pace with demand and mechanization became imperative. Although some women work under factory conditions, most housewives operate a hand flat machine sufficiently compact to be installed in the living-room or kitchen. It is still largely a cottage industry with the whole family participating—the men too in their spare time. The art of knitting patterned garments still flourishes, although the price obtained by the knitter is hopelessly inadequate considering the time spent in producing garments of this type. Fair Isle gloves, scarves and pill-box hats meet a ready demand from visitors, while an extremely popular line is machine-knitted cardigans incorporating a hand-knitted patterned yoke.

The raising of beef cattle is another important aspect of crofting, the animals being kept indoors during the winter in modern cattle sheds where they are fed largely on silage. Few crofters keep a cow for milking nowadays. It is more convenient to purchase milk as required in plastic bags from the nearest shop.

The hill dykes that used to separate each township from the heather-clad hills can still be traced as low green ridges with here and there the stump of a wooden stick standing like a monument to a system that has gone. The dry-stone dykes erected by lairds and sheep farmers during the nineteenth century still stand remarkably intact, but the older hill dykes have been replaced by wire fences that divide the landscape into a pattern of neat, geometrical figures. Crofts have been restructured as with depopulation they have gradually combined into much larger units, enabling those crofters who remain to derive a much higher income. Nevertheless there are few crofts that can support a family without a full-time job elsewhere. Fortunately there now exists a wide range of jobs which enable families to live in rural districts although the actual income may be derived from a job at Lerwick.

The old drying beaches have long been idle, and the trade in salt fish has practically gone, although each summer a few hundred barrels of salt herring are exported from the last of Lerwick's curing yards. Nowadays the most important species is haddock, which is processed in a dozen factories in several parts of the Mainland and in the islands of Burra, Whalsay, Skerries and Yell. A considerable proportion of the islands' catch finds its way to America, being exported in refrigerated vessels direct from Scalloway.

The fishing industry continues to be the most important of our traditional industries, although it is largely centralized at Lerwick, Scalloway, Whalsay, Burra, Skerries and Yell. The design of fishing boats has altered considerably, and high prices generally afford a good living, but still the lives of the fishermen are dominated by the ebb and flow of the tide, the shooting and hauling of trawl and seine, the long hours of working and the short hours of sleep. In many respects the men have to work harder nowadays than they did a hundred years ago. After the sixern was hauled ashore all expense came to an end before it was launched again, but now there is the weekly insurance payments and the hire of echosounder, Decca navigator and other equipment to meet whether the boat is fishing or tied up in port. Fishermen cannot afford to stay ashore, and hence they fish in conditions which come very near the limits of safety.

Each boat is equipped with radio, and frequent weather forecasts advise the fishermen of coming storms, giving them time to get the catch below deck and head for home as the sea responds to the rising gale. Electronic aids have made such journeys safer, but near the shore unlit headlands and submerged reefs still require the vigilance of the man at the wheel.

Although most of the larger boats have come from yards on the Scottish Mainland, in Holland and in Norway, the skill of building small boats has been retained in Shetland. Large numbers of small, undecked vessels are used for pleasure and for part-time fishing in summer, many of them the clinker-built, double-ended Shetland model that these islands have known for over a thousand years.

The building of small vessels received a boost in the 1950s and 1960s with the growing importance of lobster fishing. This is the most dangerous occupation of all. The creels are set close inshore on the sheltered side of a headland, but in Shetland the wind seldom blows from one direction for long, and the creels may have to be hauled on what has suddenly become a lee shore. In such cases the risks are high, since it takes only one strand of rope around a small boat's propeller to disable it and leave it at the mercy of the waves and the rocks.

In spite óf the tendency for modern society to congregate in towns, many people have clung to the open life of rural Shetland. Living is seldom easy, since the island industries are entirely at the mercy of the climate or of market processes and prices for fish, livestock and knitwear can tumble quite unexpectedly.

The benefits are difficult to define, and few of those who cling so tenaciously to their corner of Shetland can identify with certainty the essential ingredient that makes this island way of life attractive. For some it is the peace and quiet and the helpfulness of neighbours, for others it is the short but delightful summers, the seabirds and the seashore. The sea certainly fascinates every Shetlander. Even if he does not derive his living from the sea he is certain to live beside it, becoming aware, perhaps unconsciously, of its ebb and flow, its moods and its ever-changing appearance. For many people, however, the great attraction of Shetland is simply its distinctiveness, which is shown in its history, its customs, its music and its songs, and above all in its form of speech.

THE DIALECT TODAY

One of the factors in the decline of Norn was the absence of a written language. Norn left no literature apart from a few ballads and a few fragments of verse handed down orally until they were preserved at the end of the nineteenth century. Its successor, the Shetland dialect, however, does have a literature although it is hampered by the lack of uniformity in spelling.

One of the finest works written wholly in the dialect is *Shetland Fireside Tales* by George Stewart, which appeared in 1877. It was a humorous work, and unfortunately this characteristic was accentuated by those who sought to emulate him. The dialect was seen as a medium for comedy, and the recurring theme in subsequent works was the life style of the old Shetlander faced with a changing situation and unable to adapt to it. There followed such works as *Maunsie's Röd* by James Inkster, *Humours of a Peat Commission* by Thomas Manson, and *Lowrie* by Joseph Gray. While they certainly preserved many of the old words in their correct context, they probably harmed the dialect by regarding it solely as a vehicle for humour.

Other writers sought a wider audience by writing in English

and trying to bring to the notice of the British public the importance of Shetland and its culture. These included Jessie M. E. Saxby, W. Fordyce Clark and Peter A. Jamieson. Best known of Shetland's authors is James J. Haldane Burgess, 1863-1927, whose historical novels include *The Viking Path* which deals with the old struggle between Christianity and Norse Paganism.

Shetland has produced several poets, and although most of them have written in English this part of their work lacks distinction. When writing in the dialect, on the other hand, they achieve a remarkable cadence and ease of expression, and it is only the failure of the British public to understand the dialect that has prevented them from achieving a higher status in British literature.

Best known poet is again James J. Haldane Burgess, whose works include the highly humorous *Skranna*, in which the Devil pays a visit to an ordinary Shetland croft house inhabited by a crofter, Rasmie, and his dog. At first Rasmie is taken in by the visitor's appearance—

> A gantleman, braa-laek an weel cled afore
> Wi a lang tailly cott an a black pair o breeks,
> A sylk hat an side lichts on baid o his sheeks.

But Rasmie soon guesses the identity of his guest, and his suspicions are confirmed when he removes his gloves and Rasmie, able to study the visitor's hand for the first time, notices the fingers:

> wi da nails jöst da same as da neb o da craa.

An amusing touch is given in that Satan begins his conversation in a very proper English rather like a Shetlander who has 'been sooth' trying to impress his friends with his newly acquired proficiency. But inevitably when things go wrong Satan becomes flustered and lapses into the dialect, especially when Rasmie tries to evict him and an important part of the Satanic anatomy is caught in the door and the Devil roars:

> Ah! look oot min, Rasmie, ye're brukkin me tail.

Perhaps the best single poem in the dialect is 'Aald Maunsie's

Crø' by Basil Anderson (1861-1888)—a simple thing, like a stone enclosure for growing cabbages, yet it plays an invaluable part in the life of the community. And woven into the story is the life of Aald Maunsie himself—

> Time booed his rigg and shöre his tap
> An laid his crø in mony a slap;
> Snug-shorded by his ain hert-steyn
> He lost his senses een by een,
> Till lyin helpless laek a paet
> Nor kail nor mutton he could aet,
> Sae deed, as what we au maun dø,
> Hae we or hae we no a crø.

There are several more poets whose work lives on—James Stout Angus, famous for such poems as 'Da Kokkilurie', and 'Da Kittiwake', contained in his book of verse *Echoes from Klingrahool*, Laurence J. Nicolson, Thomas P. Ollason, John Peterson and Emily Milne. The most prolific of recent poets was Thomas A. Robertson, who wrote under the pen name Vagaland and whose work is enshrined in the book *The Collected Poems of Vagaland*. Poets who maintain the tradition today include George P. S. Peterson, Jack Renwick, Rhoda Bulter and Stella Sutherland. Many of their poems appear regularly in *The New Shetlander*, a quarterly magazine started in May 1947, and in the monthly magazine *Shetland Life*.

Inevitably the dialect has weakened considerably within the last half century, and as Dr. Jakobsen predicted, the system of education which allows only one language in the classroom meant the loss of many old words. Children came to realize that there were two forms of speech — English, which had to be used in the classroom, and the Shetland dialect used at home and while conversing in the playground. But no matter how expressive the dialect might be it was somehow considered inferior by the teachers, ministers and others who dominated the children's lives.

The ending of many of the old ways also caused the removal of a great number of words from the vocabulary. There was no need to refer to simmonds, bates o gloy and kirvies o floss when these articles were no longer being used. It was no longer necessary to 'skyle da lum' when the smoke went up the new-fangled chimney of its own accord whatever the wind's direction.

Nothing illustrates the decline of the dialect better than the study of the works of the various poets. Basil Anderson wrote of the crofting life as he knew it at the end of the nineteenth century. He refers to the practice of 'Riskin reeds an gorstie girse', which can be translated as: 'Cutting reeds, and grass growing between the fields with a sickle'. James Stout Angus in 'Da Kokkilurie' describes the daisy—'hit's head raekit up ta da sharl pin'—the lower piece of a wooden hinge.

For John Peterson the typical croft house was the neat white-washed cottage roofed with felt as he knew it during and between the wars. Things like büddies, poans and gloy had fallen out of use, but the dialect was still rich in simile and wonderfully expressive of the moods of nature. In 'Shetland' he describes the joys of searching the beaches during a storm—

> Dere I look alang da shoormil
> Among da tang an waar
> Fir barrel-scowes an battens
> An bits o brokken spar.
> Fir da muckle seas is brakkin
> In stoor laek cloods a snaa,
> An dere tales o vessels wrackin
> Wi der sails aa blaan awa.

Vagaland's Shetland was the district of Walls, a region of deep penetrating voes and numerous lochs, of tiny crofts in the valleys between rock-strewn hillsides, and his dialect is still based solidly on the old words that convey such a wealth of meaning. In 'Da Sang o da Papa Men' he describes the appearance of that lovely island of the west:

> Laek a lass at's hoidin, laachin,
> Coortit be her vooers,
> Papa sometimes lies in simmer
> Veiled wi ask an shooers;
> Dan upo da wilsom water
> Comes da scent o flooers.

He wrote of the people and their daily tasks, of the cycle of the year, of the birds and of the flowers that brightened the landscape. And always out of a simple theme easily overlooked by others, he wove a message of great profundity and of direct application to everyday life. In 'Vaigin On' he wrote of the truths learned at Sunday School and of their influence on his life:

> Da faith o single-herted men,
> Da veeshon an da draem,
> Der ballast-stanes for ony-een
> At's far an far fae hame.

He was deeply attached to the dialect, and indeed his poems illustrate accurately the vocabulary and the idioms of twentieth-century speech. As he wrote in another poem: 'Trowe wir minds wir ain aald language still keeps rinnin loak a tön.'

In an article in *The New Shetlander* not published until after his death in 1974, he declared that an attempt must be made to save the dialect before it declines too far. 'What is required now in Shetland,' he wrote, 'is a really comprehensive collection of the idiomatic phrases and expressions which are the life-blood of Shetland dialect.' He suggested that a group of interested people from all over Shetland should get together to construct a generally accepted form of dialect which could be used by Shetland writers as Ny Norsk is in Norway.

Rhoda Bulter lives in Lerwick, but a two-year period spent at Lunnasting during the Second World War made a deep impression on her and gave her a love for the crofting way of life which seems to be indispensable to a writer in the dialect. Her short poem 'Voar' expresses that almost indescribable feeling that comes over everyone in Shetland when the winter is over.

> Here an dere I can see da green paek,
> An' da midden is spread ower da rig.
> Nae langer da stirleens sit klined ower da daek,
> Dir awa finnin somewye ta bigg.
> I kin smell da reek fae a heddery fire,
> Dir a klaag a birds doon at da shore.
> A blackbird whistles fae da rüf o da byre
> An suddenly, its voar.

Rhoda Bulter takes the dialect right up to the present time, discussing such aspects of modern life as television and milk in plastic bags. In 'Observations in a Bar' she describes the scene as the patrons sit sipping their drinks.

> Dey sat aroond at peerie poalished tables,
> Someens I kent an twartree unken fok;
> Sippin perskeet-laek noo an dan fae glesses,
> For da time wis juist da back a seevin a'clock.

One gets the impression that Rhoda Bulter is not entirely at ease in a bar, and the contrast between the emancipated modern women she sees there and the women she knew on the croft is clear.

> Da weemin hardly spak abün a whisper,
> Sat dat pernyim aye fiddlin wi der gless;
> Dan reddit up dir hair or snet dir noses,
> An purled dir fags atti da plaet a ess.

In the last line one can almost visualize a woman of bygone days standing in the doorway bemused by the scene, especially the cigarettes between the women's lips and above all 'da plaet a ess' — ashtrays are a refinement that had no place in the traditional croft house.

Her parodies of nursery rhymes indicate the vivacity of her speech and also show how much of the old way of life is incorporated into crofting today.

> Come peerie Jeemie an whistle 'pun Spy.
> Da coarn's been truckit be twa unken kye,
> Da sheep is come oot o da park at da banks,
> An da aald moorit almark is broken her branks.
> Whaar, tell me whaar, can be yun boy o wirs?
> He's lyin soond asleep in a swerd o green girse.

And again—

> Da nort wind'll blaa
> And we'll hae snaa
> And whaat will da caddies dü dan, poor tings?

We'll get dem weel bül'd
Wi some hey an dry müld
Or dey'll maybe moor up in a fan poor tings.

It is important to note that in the dialect caddies have nothing
to do with golf—they are the motherless lambs that become almost family pets for a time. Again a fan is a snowdrift.

Rhoda Bulter's poems, and those of her contemporaries, are
proof that the dialect is still with us, a marvellous vehicle for
describing nature, the sea and the weather. It contains a wealth
of simile and metaphor and its rich, resonant vowels are ideal
for expressing such a wide range of meaning and indispensable
for deflating a person who thinks too highly of himself. But
it is questionable how long the present strength of the dialect
can be maintained, since children are taught at school in English, while at home they are subject to the influence of television. A generation is growing up that hears the real dialect only
occasionally, and even then with a limited vocabulary.

It is difficult to see how the dialect can survive unless steps
are taken to make young people interested in their island heritage, of which the dialect is the most tangible aspect. There is
a strong case for making Shetland studies a subject in the curriculum of every school, if only for one hour each week. There
is also the task of collecting and collating the many old words,
sayings and stories that have not yet been recorded. Each part
of Shetland has its own peculiar expressions and its own purely
local anecdotes; and unless a record is made for each part of
Shetland much will be lost. The school should play a major
role in this under the guidance of interested teachers, for the
schools, through their pupils have access to almost every house
in their respective districts, and in many cases access to the
memories of old people who were born at the end of last century. Unfortunately with each death another part of our island
heritage is lost for ever.

MUSIC, SONG AND DANCE

Music still plays a great part in the lives of Shetlanders, and
the fiddle remains the most popular musical instrument. Fiddle
tunes fall roughly into three groups—wedding tunes such as
'The Bride's Reel' from Unst, 'trowie' tunes or pieces of music

reputed to have been learned near the haunts of the trows and reel tunes. Each district has its own reel tunes with purely local titles such as 'Benigirt Hoose', 'Da Gert Lasses' or 'Behint da daeks o Voe'. Best known reel tune is probably 'Da Merry Boys o Greenland' which honours Shetland's former links with the Arctic whaling industry.

Within recent years no one had done more than Mr Thomas Anderson of Lerwick to keep alive Shetland's musical traditions. He is leader of a group known as 'The Forty Fiddlers' whose recordings are popular even outwith Shetland and whose practice sessions have become something of a tourist attraction. It was fitting that in the New Year's Honours List for 1977 Mr Anderson was awarded the M.B.E. for his services to music. Better known outside Shetland is Mr Anderson's former pupil, Aly Bain, who is in demand at international festivals of folk music and appears regularly on television.

Unlike the Western Isles, Shetland's list of traditional songs is short, since most of the old Norn ballads were lost through neglect of the language. During the past hundred years, however, several traditional dialect songs have been recorded and several poems have been set to music. In 1944 a number of people began to take an interest in Shetland music, and the Shetland Music Festival Committee made an appeal for Shetland tunes. The response was so encouraging that a sub-committee was appointed to arrange a programme of Shetland music and dances. The concert was a great success and this gave Mr Neil Matheson, then postmaster at Lerwick, the idea of forming a society with similar aims to those of An Commun Gaidhealach. The outcome was Shetland Folk Society, which has played a great part in preserving so much of the islands' cultural heritage.

In 1973 the society published a collection of Shetland songs under the title *Da Sangs at A'll sing ta Dee*. This includes old Norse ballads, traditional lullabies and spinning songs and a great number of more recent poems set to music. Many people were surprised at the volume of material available, since the book contains no fewer than sixty songs, many of them of great beauty and worthy of a much wider audience than a purely local one.

While the traditional reels, the Foula reel and the Shetland reel, date only from the late eighteenth century, there is one dance that traces its origins back to Norse times. This is the Papa Stour Sword Dance, which is similar to the ancient sword dances of the Norsemen. Those dances, however, are performed by six players, but in this case a seventh has been added and the seven dancers represent the seven saints of Christendom. The leader is St George of England, who after introductory fiddle music has been played opens the dance with a prologue before performing his own dance. Then he recites a further verse to inform the company of the entertainment that is to follow. He introduces his six companion knights—St James, St Denis, St David, St Patrick, St Anthony and St Andrew, each of whom in turn draws his sword and dances. Then the sword dance proper begins—a series of complicated movements in which the sword figures prominently culminating in the formation of a 'shield' of interlocked swords.

The Papa Stour Sword Dance is certainly one of Shetland's oldest institutions, a distinction which it shares with the festival of Up-Helly-Aa. It must be stressed, however, that in its present form the festival is comparatively modern, but its origin dates back to the time of the Norsemen and the celebrations which marked the end of the festive season—the 24th night of Yule. The festival used to be held on the 29th of January, but in 1908 it was decided to hold it instead on the last Tuesday of January, and this became the accepted day for Up-Helly-Aa.

Preparations begin many months beforehand. A Guizer Jarl, or chief guizer, is chosen and sub-committees are appointed to take care of specific activities such as the building of the galley and the making of up to 800 torches from wood and sacking. The guizers themselves are divided into squads of twelve or fourteen men, who usually make their own fancy dress in strict secrecy, each squad taking a single theme.

The final part of the preparations is the painting of the Bill— a ten-feet high, beautifully-decorated proclamation which pokes fun at local institutions, personalities and the events of the past year. It is attached to the Market Cross on the morning of Up-Helly-Aa and is eagerly scanned by those who hope or fear that their escapades may deserve a mention in the bill.

The festival takes place at night, the flames from the torches illuminating the crowds that line the streets as the galley is dragged to its burning site. The climax of the procession takes place in the King George V Playing Fields, where the torches are flung into the galley, which soon becomes a pyre as flames destroy the splendid dragon head and sparks shoot high into the sky over Lerwick.

The burning of the galley marks the end of the first part of the proceedings. Next comes the round of the dozen or so halls which each squad must visit in strict order. Here the night's revelry is held, organized by hard-working hostesses. At each hall the squad performs an act which may be a dance, a brief sketch, or a song in keeping with its theme. When this is completed the squad has the privilege of choosing the next dance.

Other old Shetland customs have diminished over the years but Up-Helly-Aa goes from strength to strength, as if all the many festivals once observed in the islands have been rolled into one dazzling extravaganza of fire, colour, music, song and dance. And through it all comes a reminder of the old Vikings whose blood still runs strongly in the veins of their Shetland descendants.

LIVING WITH OIL

In the late 1960s a new kind of vessel appeared on the fishing banks east of Shetland. But unlike the seiners and trawlers they were not interested in the shoals of fish or the bottom of the sea. Their interest lay in the rocks far below the seabed and the folds and geological structures that might conceivably contain oil. After the seismic survey vessels came the oil rigs, working under a veil of secrecy, their drills biting ever deeper into the floor of the North Sea. They recorded some minor successes, and then one day the drill of Shell's rig *Staflo* pierced the huge reservoir of oil and gas to which the company gave the name Brent after a species of Arctic goose. Almost immediately Shetland assumed a new importance, and businessmen and entrepreneurs who until then had had only the vaguest idea about Shetland's geographical position packed their bags and booked their passages north to stake their claim to a share of the expected bonanza.

First to feel the impact of oil were Shetland's harbours, which found a new role as service bases from which cement, chemicals, food and other supplies could be shipped out to the oil rigs, while Sumburgh Airport, at the southern tip of Shetland, found a new importance as the airport nearest the oilfields of the northern North Sea. And this was just the beginning, since it was clear from the magnitude of the oil discoveries that Shetland would be heavily involved in the oil industry and that a large oil storage complex would be required somewhere in the islands.

Inevitably there were those who opposed oil-related developments who if they had been able would have prevented oil being landed in Shetland. They dreaded the effects of a new industrialized society on a predominantly crofting and fishing community and feared that the islanders might be outnumbered eventually by incoming oilworkers. With the latter, it was feared, would come all the ills that have so long plagued Britain's cities, including drug addiction, vandalism, theft and even murder. Children would no longer be able to play outside without causing parental concern, and even social functions would have to stop, since village halls would be unable to cope. Environmentalists feared the loss of amenity through industrial developments on some of the most attractive parts of Shetland's coastline, and there was the constant threat of a massive oil spill with its catastrophic effects on seabirds and marine life. It was also predicted that people would forsake the traditional industries for better paid jobs with the oil companies.

Shetland suffered severely under the initial impact of oil developments, as many of its services were stretched to the limit and its roads deteriorated under the strain of heavy loads. Local industry suffered to a certain extent from the competition for labour, and a few smaller firms were forced to close down owing to the loss of one or two key men. But there were undoubted compensations, not the least of which was full employment and wages at a level never before experienced in these islands. Fortunately the major industries fared better than had been expected and proved their ability to co-exist with the new industry.

Since then Shetland has come to terms with the oil industry. In some cases developments have been directed to areas which had long suffered from neglect, and the period of construction was also one of restoration. The North harbour of Lerwick was for long disfigured with rotting jetties, unused since the herring boom, sticking out like dead fingers that the town could neither use nor shake off. Now they are gone, and in their place have come modern quays and warehouses with a constant coming and going of smart cargo vessels and the less attractive but highly efficient oil service boats.

Sumburgh Airport has been expanded considerably to cater for the increased activity, and many of Shetland's best beaches in that area are no longer the quiet restful places they used to be. But a minimum of agricultural land has been sacrificed; the crofts have been spared and there is the added bonus of work for the young people. Indeed the direction of the labour flow has been reversed, and many people now travel from as far afield as Lerwick to their jobs at Sumburgh.

Most pronounced of all are the developments at Sullom Voe, where what will soon become the largest oil terminal in Europe is being constructed. The scale of the development is colossal, yet somehow it is dwarfed by the wide curving sweep of the voe and by the bare, peat-covered headlands behind. Some villages, such as Brae and Mossbank, are expanding to accommodate the influx of workers, but others in the vicinity remain untouched. Sullom, the township that also gave its name to the voe, remains a quiet crofting area rather bemused by all the activity on the opposite shores. It is amazing how many of the old Norse names have suddenly become household words in Britain. Sullom, according to Dr Jakobsen, was *sol heimr*—a place in the sun.

Oil has certainly brought some disadvantages, but one advantage which must not be overlooked is the return of people to parts of the islands that have long suffered from depopulation, and among them are a high proportion of young people who had been forced to leave the islands through lack of employment in the past. Many of them are still not accustomed to the novelty of being able to make a living at home.

As yet there is no sign that the oil industry will destroy the more commendable aspects of the Shetland way of life. Shetland still attracts a large number of people who are tired of the rat-race in the cities, who are glad to come to a place where a man's occupation does not determine his standing in the community and where it does not influence the progress of his children at school. People can still find here a sense of freedom from the trappings of the twentieth century, and if they wish they can still fend for themselves to a great extent, growing their own vegetables, catching their own fish and cutting and drying their own fuel.

Wages are high at present and many hundreds of Shetlanders are benefiting already, yet there is a realization that this level of affluence cannot continue; that oil is only one chapter in Shetland's history; that some day the oil fields will run dry and we will be left with the land and the sea and the traditional industries of crofting, fishing and knitting. Already some people are being repelled by the affluence that is everywhere around them, anxious to return to a more simple way of life. There is a growing realization that the thrift of a past generation has much to commend it.

There is a new interest in every aspect of life in Shetland— a new awareness of the environment, and an admiration for the history of the islands and their traditions. People now realize that a study of the islands' culture enhances their sense of belonging to 'The Old Rock'. There is no room for complacency, since oil related developments could destroy much of the essential charm of these islands. On the other hand, oil could produce the jolt necessary to make us realize the importance of our heritage and how much there is that is worth saving.

Map

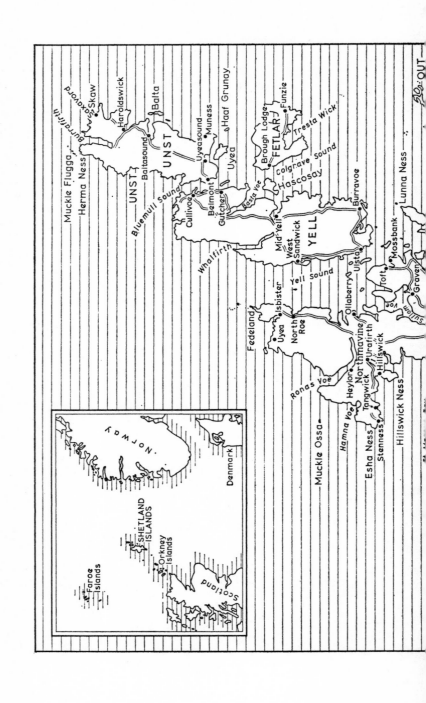

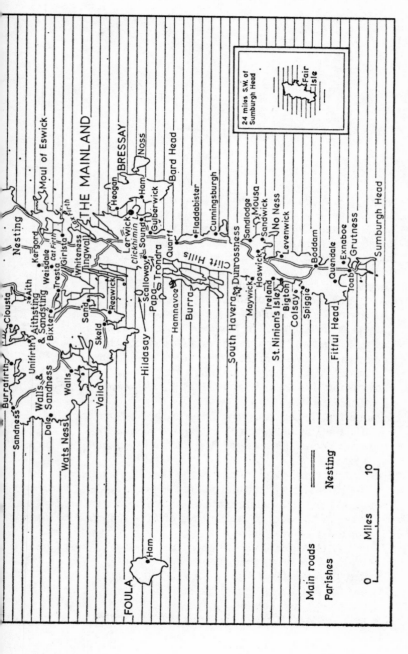

FOULA

• Ham

Burrafirth •
Sandness •
• Clousta
Walls & Unifirth • Aithsting
Dale • Sandness
Watts Ness
Walls •
Kargord
Aith •
Waisdale
Tresta • Catfirth
Girlsta •
Firth

Nesting

Moul of Eswick

THE MAINLAND

Heogan •
BRESSAY
Noss

Whiteness
Ingwall
Larwick • Ham •
Gulberwick
Bard Head

Vaila •
Skeld •
Reawick •

Sand •
Clickhimin L.
Scalloway • Sound
Papa Trondra
Quarff

Cliff Hills

• Fladdabister
• Cunningsburgh

Hildasay
Hamnavoe •
Burra •
South Havera & Dunrossness

Maywick •
Hoswick •
Sandlodge
Mousa
Sandwick
No Ness
Levenwick

St. Ninian's Isle •
Ireland •
Bigton •
Colsay •
Spiggie •
Quandale
Boddam •
Exnaboe •
Toab • Grutness
Sumburgh Head

Fitful Head

Fair Isle

24 miles S.W. of
Sumburgh Head

Main roads ————— Nesting
Parishes

0   Miles   10

Based with permission on the Ordnance Survey

Bibliography

Angus, J. S. *A Glossary of the Shetland Dialect* (Paisley 1914)

Brand, Rev J. *A Brief Description of Orkney, Zetland, Pightland Firth and Caithness* (Edinburgh 1701)

Brøgger, A. W. *Ancient Emigrants* (Oxford 1929)

Bulter, R. *Shaela* (Sandwick, Shetland 1976)

Burgess, J. J. H. *The Viking Path* (Edinburgh 1894)

Cheyne, J. R. 'Huggeranohni', *The New Shetlander*, No. 13 (1947)

Clark, W. F. *The Story of Shetland* (Edinburgh 1906)

Cluness, A. T. *The Shetland Isles* (London 1951)

Cluness, A. T. (Editor). *The Shetland Book* (Lerwick 1967)

Cowie, R. *Shetland, Description and Historical* (Aberdeen 1879)

Edmondston, A. *View of the Ancient and Present State of the Zetland Islands* Vols. I and II (Edinburgh 1809)

Edmondston, Rev B. and Saxby, J. M. E. *The Home of a Naturalist* (London 1888)

Edmondston, T. *On the Native Dyes of the Shetland Islands*, Trans. Bot. Soc., Edinburgh, Vol. 1 (1841)

Eunson, J. *Words, Phrases and Recollections from Fair Isle* (Lerwick 1976)

Evershed, H. *On the Agriculture of the Islands of Shetland*, Trans. of the Highland Agricultural Society of Scotland, Vol. 6 (1874)

Fenton, A. *Early and Traditional Cultivating Implements in Scotland*, Proc. of the Soc. of Antiquaries of Scotland, Vol. 94 (Session 1962–63)

Gifford, T. *Historical Description of the Zetland Islands* (1786 reprinted Edinburgh 1879)

Goodlad, C. A. *Shetland Fishing Saga* (Lerwick 1971)

Goudie, G. *The Celtic and Scandinavian Antiquities of Shetland* (Edinburgh and London 1904)

Goudie, G. (Editor) *Diary of the Reverend John Mill* (Edinburgh 1889)

Halcrow, Capt A. *The Sail Fishermen of Shetland* (Lerwick 1950)

Hibbert, S. *Description of the Shetland Islands* (Edinburgh 1822, reprinted Lerwick 1891)

Jakobsen, J. *The Dialect and Place Names of Shetland* (Lerwick 1897)

Jakobsen, J. *An Etymological Dictionary of the Norn Language in Shetland* (London and Copenhagen 1928–32)

Jakobsen, J. *The Place Names of Shetland* (London and Copenhagen 1936)

Jamieson, P. A. *The Viking Isles* (London 1933)

Jamieson, P. A. *Letters on Shetland* (Edinburgh 1949)

Linklater, E. *Orkney and Shetland* (London 1965)

Low, G. *A Tour Through Orkney and Shetland in 1774* (Kirkwall 1879)

MacWhirter, A. *The Early Days of Independentism and Congregationalism in the Northern Isles* of Scotland. Records of the Scottish Church History Society (1966)

Manson, T. *Lerwick During the Last Half Century* (Lerwick 1923)

Marwick, E. W. *The Folklore of Orkney and Shetland* (London 1975)

Mitchell, C. E. *Up-Helly-Aa* (Lerwick 1948)

Moffat, W. Shetland: *The Isles of Nightless Summer* (London 1934)

Napier Commission. Evidence taken by H.M. Commissioners of Inquiry into the conditions of the crofters and cottars in the Highlands & Islands of Scotland, Vol. 2 (Edinburgh 1884)

New Statistical Account of Scotland. Shetland Islands (Edinburgh 1841)

Nicolson, J. R. *Shetland* (Newton Abbot 1972)

Nicolson, J. R. *Shetland and Oil* (London 1975)

O'Dell, A. C. *The Historical Geography of the Shetland Islands* (Lerwick 1939)

Rampini, C. *Shetland and the Shetlanders* (Kirkwall 1884)

Reid, J. T. *Art Rambles in Shetland* (Edinburgh 1869)

Robertson, T. A. *The Collected Works of Vagaland* (Lerwick 1975)

Robertson, T. A. and Graham, J. J. *The Grammar and Usage of the Shetland Dialect* (Lerwick 1953)

Roussell, A. *Norse Building Customs in the Scottish Isles* (London and Copenhagen 1934)

Russel, Rev J. *Three Years in Shetland* (Paisley 1887)

Sandison, C. *The Sixareen and her Racing Descendants* (Lerwick 1954)

Sandison, W. *Remnants of the Norn* (Lerwick 1953)

Saxby, J. M. E. *Shetland Traditional Lore* (Edinburgh 1932)

Shetland Folk Society. *Shetland Folk Book*, Vols. 1–6 (Lerwick 1947–76)

Shirreff, J. *General View of the Agriculture of the Shetland Islands* (Edinburgh 1814)

Sinclair, Sir J. *The (Old) Statistical Account of Scotland* (Edinburgh 1791–99)

Smith, J. *A Description of the island of Shetland and the fishing thereabout* (1633). MacFarlane's Geographical Collections Vol. 3

Smith, Rev J. A. *Sinclair Thomson the Shetland Apostle* (Lerwick 1969)

Spence, J. *Shetland Folk Lore* (Lerwick 1899)

Stewart, G. *Shetland Fireside Tales* (Edinburgh 1877)

Truck Commission. 'Report of the Commission appointed to enquire into the Truck System Together with Minutes of Evidence.' Vol. 2, Minutes of Evidence (Edinburgh 1872)

Tudor, J. R. *The Orkneys and Shetland* (London 1883)

Index

Aberdeen, 109, 115, 172, 174

Accidents, 112, 160, 165, 170, 173, 175

Agriculture, 17, 23, 35, 53, 54–6; agricultural implements, 60–3, 176; see also Crofting

Aithsting, 21, 92

Alting, 19

Anderson, Arthur, 99

Anderson, Basil, 184, 185

Anderson, Thomas, 189

Angus, James S., 184, 185

Annexation by Scotland, 19, 38

Antinsmas, 70

Archaeology, 17–9

Augury, 141, 145, 166

Bain, Aly, 189

Baltasound, 34, 74, 93, 113, 122, 175

Barns, 63, 164

Baskets, 41, 64, 65, 89, 93

Beaches, 51, 64, 69, 83, 105, 106, 109, 114, 118, 159, 160, 180

Beds, 73, 76, 77, 80

Beest, 80

Beltane, 143

Bere, 54–6, 63, 66, 79, 80

Bertie, 136

Bible, 20, 39, 77, 155

Birds, 42, 65, 66, 138, 141, 145, 192; as food, 83

Blaand, 80, 107

Blacksmith, 76, 79, 88

Blight, 68

Board for the Relief of Highland Destitution, 28

Boatbuilding, 103, 115, 181

Boats, see Fourern, Sixern, Yoal

Bogel day, 141

Bohemian Girl, 115

Bonfires, 143, 153, 191

Borrowing days, 142

Brae, 179, 193

Bread, 35, 79, 84, 109, 142, 164

Bressay, 29

Bressay Sound, 21, 22, 143

Brochs, 17

Bronze Age, 17, 102

Brora, 101

Brownie, 129, 157

Bryden, Dr J., 88

Building techniques, 71–5, 87, 171, 176

Bulter, Rhoda, 184, 186–8

Bundling, 161

Burgess, J. J. Haldane, 154, 183

Burra, 92, 121, 142, 154, 174, 180, 183

Burstane, 80, 142, 146

Buss, 21, 30, 112

Butter, 80, 129, 132

Byres, 56, 59, 62, 69, 171

Caaing whales, 30, 104, 119–21

Cabbages, 41, 54, 56, 80

Caithness, 38

Candlemas, 147
Carding, 98, 161
Cattle, 41, 43, 56, 61, 62, 84, 180
Celts, 17
Childbirth, 155
Children, 46, 84, 155–60, 192
Christianity, 18, 20, 127, 146, 155, 183
Christmas, 140, 146–53
Churches, 18, 32, 33, 35, 127, 140, 147, 149
Churchmen, 19, 20, 127, 146, 155, 183
Churns, 80, 129, 132
Claith, 97
Clearances, 23
Clickhimin, 94
Clift Hills, 57, 168
Clift Sound, 92
Clark, W. F., 183
Climate, 42, 54, 64, 70, 117, 119, 138, 142, 182
Clothing, 98, 108, 180
Cod, 22, 83, 105, 108, 112, 113, 135, 174
Cooking utensils, 78, 79, 129
Coir, 89
Commons, *see* Scattalds
Communications, 26, 30, 33, 34, 109, 115, 172
Congregational Church, 33
Courtship, 161
Court of Session, 168
Cowie, Dr R., 35
Crime, 192
Crøs, 41, 67, 179
Crofter fishermen, 17, 22–4, 27, 110, 123, 165, 174, 175
Crofters Commission, 56
Crofters Holdings (Scotland) Acts, 25, 58, 86, 121, 168
Crofting, 50–70, 142, 144, 169–70, 179, 180, 186
Cromwell, Oliver, 21
Cullivoe, 121, 175
Cunningsburgh, 120, 168
Customs officers, 30, 114
Cycling, 173

Dancing, 29, 38, 146, 148, 153, 161, 164, 189, 190
Davis Straits, 29, 113
Death, 27, 112, 162, 166, 170, 176
Delting, 24, 150
Denmark, 19, 102
Depopulation, 170, 175, 176
Dialect, 38–49, 182–8
Disasters, 112, 170, 176
Dowell, Anton, 27
Drink, 31, 79, 80, 84, 85, 96, 110, 148, 162, 164, 167
Drifter, sail, 121–3, 174; steam drifter, 174; motor drifter, 174; *see also* Buss
Driftwood, 33, 88, 160
Duncan, W., 115
Dunrossness, 31, 33, 57, 62, 63, 72, 78, 89, 94, 102, 105, 169
Dutch fishermen, 21, 30, 31, 44, 99, 112, 121, 143, 181
Dyes, 99, 179
Dykes, 50, 53, 57, 65, 69, 97, 180

Earldom of Orkney and Shetland, 18
Earl of Zetland, 34
Easter, 142
Edinburgh, 168, 170
Edmondston, Dr A., 32
Edmondston, Dr L., 26
Education, 45, 158, 159
Emigration, 24, 170, 175, 176
Enclosure of farmland, 54
English language, 37, 45, 183, 184
Evershed, H., 55, 61, 73
Evictions, *see* Clearances

Fair Isle, 53, 100, 102, 103, 105, 170, 173; knitwear, 100, 180
Falkland Islands, 89
Fallow, 54–6
Family life, 28, 29, 46–9, 83–6, 155–67
Famine, 21, 28, 79, 118, 169
Faroe Islands, 30, 38, 39, 113, 114

Fedeland, 106, 107, 109
Fetlar, 23, 55, 93, 98, 106, 130, 150, 179
Fiddlers, 29, 126, 148, 161, 188–90
Fishcuring, 22, 82, 106, 109, 122, 170, 180
Fishing grounds, 21, 42, 105, 113, 115, 175, 181
Fishing industry: early commercial, 22, 105; haaf fishing, 66, 68, 106–12; haddock fishing, 115–7, 135, 144, 175; herring fishing, 21, 28, 121–3, 143, 174–6, 180; modern industry, 117, 180–2; smack fishery, 30, 83, 113–5; subsistence fishery, 82, 117–21
Fishing tenure, 22
Fitful Head, 117
Fladdabister, 87
Flowers, 66, 74, 99, 138, 144
Fodder, 52, 56, 69
Fogrigarth, 80
Food, 33, 35, 75, 79–83, 109, 119, 146, 164
Football, 147, 148, 150
Foudes, 19
Foula, 33, 35, 36, 39, 83, 87, 104, 150, 173, 190
Fourern, 104
France, 27; influence on dialect, 44
Free Church, 33, 34, 127
Furniture, 75–8, 85

Germany, 22, 99, 122; influence on dialect, 44; trade with, 22, 99, 122
Gokstad ship, 102
Goodlad, L., 115
Goudie, John, 29
Grand Hotel, 35
Grassland, 50–3, 55, 179
Gray, Joseph, 182
Grazing, 50, 52, 53, 56, 58, 179
Gregorian calendar, 140
Grimista, 19
Gue, 29
Guizing, 149, 151, 152, 164, 190

Haaf Grunay, 33, 53
Haddock, 82, 115–7, 175, 177, 180
Haddock boat, 92, 115–7, 175
Hagra, 52
Hairst, 68, 144
Halibut, 82, 108, 135
Hallowmas, 80, 115, 160
Hamnavoe, 172, 179
Hanseatic merchants, 22, 99
Harrows, 61, 145
Hay, 53, 56, 67, 179
Hay & Co., 115
Health, 26, 166, 171
Herring, 21, 28, 82, 83, 107, 113, 115, 118, 121–3, 143, 174
Hibbert, Dr S., 30, 32, 59, 73, 74, 77, 80, 83, 87, 90, 97, 99, 109, 110, 127, 130
Highland Society of Scotland, 57
Hildasay, 92
Hildina Ballad, 39
Hillswick, 121, 127, 172
Holland, *see* Dutch fishermen
Hoswick, 168
Housing, 62, 71–86, 170–2, 176
Hunter, Peter, 29

Iceland, 113
Immigration, 18, 20, 21, 40, 177
Ingram family, 33, 127
Inkster, James, 182
Inverness, 101
Iron Age, 17, 102

Jakobsen, Dr J., 39, 45, 97, 178, 184, 193
Jamieson, Peter, 164, 183
Jarmson, Laurence, 24
Johnsmas, 21, 66, 106, 143
Julian calendar, 140

Kate, 34
Kilns, 63, 87
Kirk session, 33
Knitting, 28, 57, 98–101, 177, 179, 180

Lairds, 19–24, 26–8, 35, 53, 93, 121, 148, 165, 168, 169
Lambing, 66
Lammas, 80, 88, 144
Lamps, 76, 77, 88
Land tenure, 19, 22
Leisk, Joseph, 120
Leith, 79, 115
Lerwick, 22, 28, 30, 31, 35, 87, 92, 113, 122, 150–4, 172, 174, 180, 190, 192
Levenwick, 29, 31, 169
Liberal party, 25
Lichens, 99
Lighthouses, 170, 172
Limestone, 87
Ling, 22, 42, 82, 83, 105, 108, 112, 133, 135
Living conditions, see Housing
Lizzie, 137
Lobster, 181
Low, George, 39, 81, 112

Magic, 131, 132
Manure, 53, 55, 57, 67
Marriage, 29, 48, 163–5
Manson, Thomas, 154, 182
Martinmas, 126, 144
Matheson, Neil, 189
Meat, 80–82, 145, 146
Merchant Navy, 27, 32, 151, 170, 174
Merchants, 27, 107, 111, 165
Methodist Church, 33
Michaelmas, 80
Milk, 56, 80, 84, 129
Mill, Rev J., 30, 57
Mills, 94–7, 129, 176; see also Querns
Milne, Emily, 184
Moar, Laurence, 116
Moar, Peter, 150
Mitchell, Sir A., 98
Monsters, 136, 137
Morning Star, 137
Monarch, 137
Motor cars, 173
Music, 29, 126, 148, 161, 188–90

Napoleonic Wars, 26, 33
Neill, Patrick, 82
Nelson, George, 142
Neolithic, 77, 102
Nesting, 130
'New' calendar, 140
New Shetlander, The, 150, 184
New Statistical Account, 31, 57
New Year's Day, 149, 150
Nicolson, J., 33
Nicolson, L. J., 184
Njuggle, 129, 157
Norsemen, 18, 19, 50, 97, 102, 124, 146, 183; Norse influence, 18, 19, 29, 40, 153, 178, 191; Norse language (Norn), 37, 38, 40–46, 134, 158, 178
Northmavine, 21, 42, 55, 61, 106, 109, 112
Norway, 37, 40, 97, 104, 181, 186; see also Norsemen

Oats, 54–6, 63, 66, 79, 169
Ockrigert, right of, 69
Oil (fish liver), 76, 78, 82, 111, 119; in peat, 90; North Sea, 17, 177, 191–4
'Old' calendar, 140, 149, 150
Old Statistical Account, 31, 55, 57, 61, 109
Ollason, T. P., 184
Orkney, 18, 27, 114, 170
Out Skerries, 20, 92, 101, 174, 180

Papa, 92
Papa Stour, 92, 118, 121, 130, 142, 150, 175, 176, 190
Papil, 18
Patronymics, 20
Peat, 21, 59, 66, 89–94, 106
Peterson, George P. S., 184
Peterson, John, 184
Picts, 18
Pigs, 59
Piltocks, 42, 82, 118
Ploughs, 60, 61, 176

Ponies, 58, 59, 62, 93, 97, 169, 173, 176
Potatoes, 54, 65, 66, 67, 79, 80, 169
Poultry, 59, 60, 62, 66
Press Gang, 26, 27
Prince Consort, 34
Proverbs, 47–9

Quarff, 27
Queen's Hotel, 35
Quendale, 73
Querns, 63, 78

Ranselman, 19, 32
Reawick, 113
Reestit mutton, 82, 176
Reid, J., 34, 35, 149, 150
Religion, 18, 20, 34, 127, 140, 146, 155, 183
Renwick, J., 184
Riddles, 45–7
Roads, 26, 28, 169, 173
Robertson, T. A., 184, 185, 186
Roman Catholic Church, 20, 140, 147, 149
Ronas Voe, 175
Ropes, 71, 84, 89
Rotation of crops, 54–6
Royal Navy, 26, 151; *see also* Press Gang
Run rig system, 51, 53, 55, 179
Russia, 122

Sabbath observance, 32, 33, 34
Saithe, 42, 82, 105, 118, 144, 165
Salt, 113, 115
Salt fish, *see* Fishcuring
Salt meat, 81, 82, 176
Salt tax, 22
Sand, 120
Sandness, 122, 173, 179
Sandsting, 21
Sanitary inspectors, 171
Satan, 127, 183

Saxby, Jessie M. E., 126, 146, 153, 158, 183
Scalloway, 19, 21, 22, 92, 113, 121, 127, 174, 181
Scattalds, 24, 52, 58, 65, 179
Schools, 158, 159
Scots, 19, 20, 62, 121, 122; language, 37 38, 39, 43
Scott, Sir Walter, 96
Scousburgh, Ward of, 58
Scythes, 61, 62
Sea lore, 132–7
Seals, 33, 119, 130
Seamen, 27, 32, 86, 151, 170, 174
Seaweed, 64, 69, 83
Sheep, 23, 41, 53, 54, 57, 58, 66, 69, 81, 101, 138, 169, 179; earmarks, 58, 179
Shellfish, 83, 107, 113, 116, 119, 159, 181
Shetland Agricultural Society, 55
Shetland Folk Society, 189
Shetland News, The, 150, 173
Shipwrecks, 29, 86, 160
Sieves, 78
Sillocks, 42, 82, 118, 144, 165
Simmermill Day, 66, 142
Sinclair families, 20, 21
Sixern, 26, 92, 104, 106–12, 121, 137, 181
Skeld, 150
Skeos, 81, 82, 131
Smacks, 112–15; *see also* Drifters
Smith, J., 38
Smuggling, 30, 31, 114
Soapstone, 87
Society for the Regulation of Servants and Reformation of Manners, 32
Society of Friends, 79, 169
Sound, 74, 172, 179
Spades, 60, 62, 65
Spain, 100, 114
Spiggie, 117
Spinning, 28, 98, 179
Standen, E., 99
Stenness, 106
Stewart earls, 19
Stewart, George, 182

Stone Age, 17, 87
Stromness, 114
Sullom, 193
Sullom Voe, 17, 193
Sumburgh, 17, 19, 192, 193
Sumburgh Head, 102
Superstitions, 124–39
Surnames, 20
Swan, 29

Taboo words, 134–6
Tar barrels, 151–3
Tea, 84, 85, 96
Temperance, 31
Thomson, S., 33
Threshing, 63, 69
Timber, 71, 88
Tingwall, 19, 26, 55, 57, 142
Tourism, 35, 36
Toys, 157
Tractors, 176, 179
Transport, see Communications
Trawler, 175
Tresta, 74
Trondra, 92
Trout, 144, 160
Trows, 124–7, 132, 146, 157, 188
Truck Commission, 24
Tudor, J. R., 31, 35, 36, 99, 102
Turnips, 55, 56
Tushkar, 89
Tweed, 97

Udal law, 19, 38
Unifirth, 30
Unst, 18, 31, 33, 37, 41, 45, 78, 81,
    106, 126
Up-Helly-Aa, 149, 152, 153, 154,
    190, 191
Uyea Isle, 33
Uyeasound, 122

Vagaland, 184–6
Ve Skerries, 130
Victoria, H.R.H. Queen, 99
Vikings, see Norsemen
Visecks, 38
Vivda, 81
Voar, 65, 141, 186
Voe, 113

Wadmel, 97
Wales, Prince of, 100
Walker, John, 23
Walls, 121, 171, 175, 185
Wars, 26, 27, 33, 86, 176
Weather lore, 138, 139, 142
Weaving, see Tweed
Weisdale, 23
West Burrafirth, 21, 27
Whalfirth, 121
Whaling, 22, 27, 29, 30, 104, 119–
    21, 136, 168
Whalsay, 20, 92, 101, 112, 115, 116,
    142, 173, 174, 180
Williamson, Andrew, 135
Windows, 73
Winnowing, 63, 69
Winter, 28, 29, 69, 70
Winter Sunday, 145
Witches, 127–9, 132, 143
Wool, 28, 41, 57, 58, 67, 97, 101,
    170, 179

Yell, 20, 24, 28, 42, 83, 106, 135,
    137, 150, 171, 180
Yoal, 102–4
Yule, 29, 80, 146–8, 150–3

Zetland County Council, 169, 170
Zetland Cycling Club, 173
Zetland, Earl of, 24